Oh No!
It's Local
Rock and Roll

...but I like it!

Oh No! It's Local Rock and Roll

...but I like it!

A FOND LOOK BACK AT THE ROOTS OF ROCK AND ROLL IN EXETER AND EAST DEVON

Barry Sowden

HALSGROVE

First published in Great Britain in 2003

British Library Cataloguing-in-Publication Data
A CIP record for this title is available from the British Library

ISBN 1 84114 298 0

HALSGROVE

Halsgrove House
Lower Moor Way
Tiverton, Devon EX16 6SS
Tel: 01884 243242
Fax: 01884 243325
email: sales@halsgrove.com
website: www.halsgrove.com

Printed and bound in Great Britain by CPI Bath Press, Bath

Contents

FOR RONNIE GRAHAM

Music, when soft voices die,
Vibrates in the memory;
                    Shelley, 1821

Original drawing by Ronnie's son Gary

Foreword

This is the second book written by Barry Sowden recounting the history of local rock and roll in its many forms. The first, published in 2002, was about the bands and musicians of Mid Devon, with Tiverton as the epicentre. Such was the interest shown in the results of that labour of love that Barry's publisher, Halsgrove, asked him to do the same for Exeter and its surrounding area.

Barry is an enthusiast in all sorts of directions: collecting model lorries and musical instruments of all types, being an apprentice practitioner of the bagpipes and lifelong follower of the fortunes of Bugle FC (don't ask), are just some of his eclectic pastimes. But his ability to ferret out great rafts of apparently unconnected anecdotes and photographs and sort them into a highly readable and interesting book has really grabbed him by the truss rod.

Educated at Tiverton Grammar School where he started as an eleven-year-old in 1959, Barry soon found that the music he had learned even earlier, playing trombone in the Salvation Army Band, could be expanded. It was not long before he, along with lads of similar outlook, formed themselves into a 'beat group', The Avengers. It was in that environment that his never-ending love affair with popular music blossomed.

Nowadays, having gone through the whole gamut of residencies and one-nighters all over Devon with his second major band, Nashville Skyline, Barry amuses himself with a few local outings amongst his many friends, often playing steel guitar, but still with his trusty Strat handy, just in case someone asks for a piece by The Shadows or The Ventures.

Once Barry had committed himself to his publisher's request he enlisted the help of David 'Dan'l' Wood, his henchman-in-chief for the first book, and Bob Jarvis, bass player of many years who seems to know everyone in and around the music scene. Bob and Dan'l have both worked hard to keep Barry supplied with raw material, red wine and cigarettes, and together they have made quite a team.

There is no doubt that every musician mentioned in this book who can lay hands on a copy (sadly there are some who have not reached this part of the score) will find it difficult to put down. Not only that, but the hundreds, or I suppose thousands now that we're talking about the big city down the river, of people who grew up listening, dancing, and forming memories and relationships to their music will also find it an irresistible read.

And when it comes to a celebratory night together, as we had in Tiverton in

November 2002, those present will never forget an occasion full of warmth, rekindled friendships, and sounds they never expected to hear again. That's what music does for us, the performers and the would-be performers, for we are all one or the other. Thank you Barry and the team for helping us share it all again.

Geoff Bulley
Drummer
March 2003

Geoff Bulley

Acknowledgements

Carol and Vince Adey, Andrew Barnes, Mike 'Gribbles' Beckett, Margaret and Martin Blythe, Julie and John Bridges, Vivienne and Alan Bryant, Jill and Geoff Bulley, Rich Burns, Mrs Sue Carr, Mrs Betty Collins, Theresa and Mick Collins, Maureen and Dave Cox, Teresa and Terry Denning, Jacky and Mike Emery, Di and Peter Evans, John Ffoulkes, Gary Graham, Jean Graham, Violet and Ron Ginger, Neil Govier, Christine and Dave Green, Una and Jane Greenhalgh, June and John Greenslade, Sue and John Gregory, Maureen and Alan Haydon, Wendy and Ray Hill, Derek Holmes, Bridget and Graham Isaac, Mrs Joan Jarvis, Mike Lloyd, Julie and Dave Mulvihill, John Orton, Marion and Tony Osborne, Vic Palmer, Marjorie and Doug Parish, Sue and Mike Parr, Robin Phillips, John Portley, Doug Robertson, Peter Slater, Mary and Dave Smale, Tony Smythe, Pat Titley, Heather and Dave Vincent, John West, Gareth Whitehead, Sue 'five-star cuppa' and Tom Willmott, Bernice and Martin Wood.

SPECIAL THANKS

I am indebted to my great friend 'Bobbity' Bob Jarvis the laughing pixie, pictured here, for his invaluable assistance in researching this book.

Bob – or BJ as he is more commonly known, has been a professional musician since 1967, and his bass-playing skills are highly regarded. He is an honest, likeable chap, and from a purely personal and perhaps selfish standpoint, he is extremely computer literate. Were it not so, this book would have foundered halfway through The Corvettes' biography!

My thanks are also extended to David 'Dan'l' Wood – the other member of the research team and the former manager of the very popular Starfires. Hugely instrumental in researching the Mid Devon version of this book, Dan'l has been involved with this work in a lesser capacity owing to ill health, but his input has nevertheless been of immense help.

And finally, to the lady who has occupied the same house as I for the past thirty-four years and always seems to know when I'm thirsty – which is handy! My wife Mary... thank you dear.

Bob Jarvis

MUM AND DAD

Musicians have in the past thrown television sets out of hotel bedrooms and then wrecked the room completely; driven transit vans into swimming pools; picked flowers from garage forecourts, having forgotten their wife's birthday, and all manner of other anti-social habits. And people say, 'Well, it's how they were brought up isn't it, I blame the parents.' What a load of codswallop!

Granted, parents do occasionally say the strangest things to their musical offspring which doubtless confuses them, 'If you don't turn that noise down, you'll get a *wing* under the ear from your father when he gets home.' Whereupon, the budding guitarist, drummer, saxophonist etc. nervously awaits his Dad's arrival, concerned that he is going to develop a feathered appendage in the aural area.

Hands up all those who think, or thought, the world of their parents. OK, my left hand's up as well (I'm typing with my right), so that makes it unanimous.

They raised us, fed us, clothed us, and more importantly where the majority of musicians are concerned, they bought our first instruments.

They could not possibly have imagined the volume that can be generated by a 10-watt practice amplifier, a drum-kit, or a saxophone with a half-decent reed, powered by a young set of lungs.

Thank you Mum and Dad.

Introduction

While governments concern themselves with trifling issues like the current economic climate and world peace, young boys and girls are at this very moment, staring at the guitar, keyboard, saxophone, or whichever they were given for Christmas, and wondering if they will ever learn to play it.

As I write it is early 2003. Firemen are limbering up for strike action while servicemen and women of the United Kingdom look set to find themselves part of a coalition force in the invasion of Iraq. It is raining heavily, and there are Easter eggs in the shops. The latter apart, there are two things to which the author is looking forward: firstly, the completion of this book, and secondly, to being advised by the parents, or grandparents of any child alluded to in the first paragraph, that the youngster has managed to produce a recognisable tune from their chosen instrument.

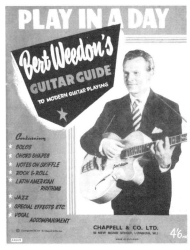

The definitive guitar tutor

From the dawn of time, music has captured the imagination of children, regardless of age, race and creed. I have spoken to countless musicians during the writing of both this, and my previous book – and am still undecided as to whether it was easier, or more difficult to learn to play a musical instrument in the 1940s and 50s, compared to the present day.

Even in the mid-50s, there were precious few teach-yourself books, and household budgets would not normally allow the provision of professional tuition. It was usually, therefore, left to the school's music teacher to teach the young boy or girl the rudiments of music. This would invariably involve the repetitive singing of the tonic sol-fa, Doh, Ray, Me, Fah and so on by the entire class, when all the young pupils really wanted to do was belt out some skiffle on a guitar or drum-kit.

There were children of course who were fortunate in having a friend, or family member who could play the guitar or some other instrument, and who was willing to pass his or her knowledge on. Some young people became members of those two laudable organisations, the Salvation Army and the Boys' Brigade, and were taught to both read and appreciate music, although from memory, neither organisation played much skiffle.

Nowadays, in addition to an abundance of professional tuition, there are manuals aplenty, video cassettes and even computer programmes available to the budding musician.

Whereas the child of yesteryear required only a cheap Spanish guitar to be able to emulate Lonnie Donegan or Wally Whyton, today's would-be pop star or starlet acquires a mini-disc or compact disc player, and a large handful

Geoff Crozier

of professionally produced studio-quality backing tracks with which to sing or play along.

A friend of mine, Geoff Crozier, in his day a peerless guitarist, once said, 'If you can play any musical instrument, you will never be without friends.' Geoff's statement is as true today as it ever was.

When the skiffle craze reached Britain from the United States, teenagers loved it. It had a lot more go in it than the 'rubbish' that mum and dad listened to on the wireless, and it was easy to play; most songs could be adequately performed using only two or three chords. Skiffle groups sprang up in schools everywhere. When it was discovered that a boy previously accused of standing in for the village idiot on his day off could play a guitar or a banjo, mandolin or drums, the lad became an instant hit with his classmates.

Many of the highly talented and successful rock outfits featured in this book evolved from skiffle groups, Gary Kane and the Tornadoes and The Graded Grains to mention but two. Musicians who progressed into traditional dance orchestras, and men such as John Portley, who went on to become agents, impresarios and club owners, all played acoustic guitar, tea-chest bass, or a kit of drums that would have been better placed on a shelf in the science museum.

Born and educated in Exeter, and a member of The Crescent City Stompers jazz band, John played an integral part in the development of the Exeter and East Devon music scene. Already an accomplished trumpet player, he left school at sixteen and joined his father's accountancy business, Portley-Lethbridge, as an articled clerk. John could now play *with* numbers from 9am to 5pm, and play *jazz* numbers in the evenings.

The Stompers boasted some fine musicians during the lifetime of the band. There was John of course, who eventually became a virtuoso on the trombone, trumpet player Bill Lowden, clarinettist Mike Mayer, banjoists Roger Hall and Geoff Cole – who was also an extremely competent trombone player – double bassists Larry Hill and Ray Newton, and among many drummers Geoff Sleeman – a lad from Dawlish – and a young man named Maurice Price.

Maurice had moved to Exeter from London, and had listened to The Stompers at the Royal British Legion Club in Little Castle Street. Introducing himself, he stated that he was a drummer, and expressed his willingness to help out, if and when required. His offer was taken up on many occasions, he and John Portley became great friends and he eventually became the band's permanent drummer.

When The Stompers were not performing at the Royal Albert Hall in London for the Festival of Jazz, or at the Bath, Ringwood, and other notable festivals, they would book a hall in the Exeter or Torquay area, and promote their own

Ron Ginger, 1972

The Maurice Price Band at Tiffany's

dances. These self-runs were always well supported, but Maurice and John felt that The Stompers needed to update their style, and get 'with it'!

Later, with clarinet and soprano-saxophone player Ron Ginger and two further 'imports' from the South East, the two men formed The Jazz Cavaliers and promptly got with it. Lest you, gentle reader, think that you have mistakenly purchased a book detailing the history of jazz in Exeter and East Devon, I should perhaps explain that The Jazz Cavaliers, with a few changes in personnel, subsequently became The Maurice Price Band – of which more later.

Whilst John Portley had left the accountancy business quite soon after qualifying, and had dabbled in various forms of self-employment – from selling hotdogs at the Exeter Speedway track, to a meals-on-wheels service quaintly named Uncle Sam's Foodrunners, when it came to promoting dances there were none better.

Paradoxically, the success of these Portley/Price events inspired John to leave the Cavaliers, a departure, which was noted by that august pop publication *Melody Maker*. The procurement of suitable premises for these functions, however, was becoming increasingly difficult. Exeter City Council had placed restrictions on both the Civic (City) and St George's halls, which governed the number of times that the venues were booked by the same organisation. In 1964, John rented a former tea and grocery warehouse on the Quay in Exeter, which he called, perhaps not too surprisingly, the Quay Club. Although primarily a discotheque, live bands like The Empty Vessels were inevitably to be seen at some point during the evening.

Four years later John Portley acquired the adjacent space, and, together with friends and a skilled labour force, created Tiffany's. John's choice of name for the new venture was not without controversy. He had 'borrowed' the name from a chain of clubs owned by the massive Mecca group who, unbeknown to John, had recently acquired premises in Exeter. The late Eric Morley, chairman of the Mecca group and the man responsible for the BBC television series 'Come Dancing' and the glitzy Miss World pageants, was apparently 'choked' when the authorities forbade him from using the name Tiffany's for his Exeter club, and hence the Riverside Club got its name.

The Jazz Cavaliers, now The Maurice Price Band, were uprooted from the

Exonian Entertainment proudly presents…

The Redhills Skiffle Group, clockwise from top: Gordon Clark, Tony Madge, Len Burgess, Albert White, Tony Smythe, Alfie Richardson

'Make a Star' contest at the Civic Hall, Exeter

Caprice Club, sited below the Rougemont Hotel in Queen Street, Exeter, and engaged as the resident band at Tiffany's, a spot they held for many years. Maurice himself retired from the band in 1980, and sold his beloved Buddy Rich drum-kit to the man to whom this book is dedicated, the much-loved and respected Ronnie Graham. Maurice Price passed away in 1982, having helped countless musicians to further their careers.

Together with his business partner Jurgen Ethridge, John Portley went from strength to strength. Shortly after his acquisition of Tiffany's, further premises, just off South Street, were renovated and became the Bag of Nails Club (subsequently named Bosuns). The shrewd businessmen also purchased the '400' Ballroom and the Harbour Steakhouse, which became the Compass Club, in Torquay. Live music was a feature in all three clubs, and there can be few local bands in East, Mid, or South Devon that did not regularly appear in at least one of them.

By the mid-60s, traditional jazz and the big-band sound, although still possessing a die-hard following, was essentially history. Skiffle groups such as The Bobcats, The Riversiders, The Spartans, and The Redhills skiffle group had long since been forgotten, and their members were now playing with bands such as The Harlequins, The Mustangs, and The Midnight Blues. Incredible though it may seem, there were sufficient bookings for all the outfits in the Exeter and East Devon area. Village halls, youth clubs, hotels and holiday camps all reverberated to the sound of rock and roll.

In addition to headlining their own dances, the boys from Devon were often given the opportunity to support professional acts. Venues such as Devonshire House in the University of Exeter, the ABC Cinema, Exmouth Pavilion and, as previously mentioned, the Civic and St George's halls, regularly played host to some of the best-known British chart-toppers touring the country at the time.

Neither were the local musicians' appearances confined to the United Kingdom. By courtesy of entertainment agencies such as Starline, owned and administered by Brian Roberts, Lionel Digby's LMD organisation in Torquay, and the Argus agency in Seaton, dreams of touring Europe were realised – although for many of the bands, the grass was definitely not greener on the other side.

Starline Entertainments

Doubtless I am biased when I make reference to the music of the late 50s and 60s, but to all those charitable organisations who are constantly running jumble, table-top and car-boot sales to aid their worthwhile causes, might I suggest that you hire a hall somewhere, book a band and insist that they play music from these two decades, stand back and take the money.

LMD Entertainments

This book has been written as a tribute to the boys and girls, men and women, who provided the music and entertainment in Exeter and East Devon from the early 50s to the late 70s and beyond. Those were the days when a young man would ask a young lady to accompany him to a dance, call for her, resplendent in a suit and tie and highly polished shoes, and reassure her dubious parents by promising that – like Cinderella – the young miss would be returned to her home by midnight, or immediately after the function. Unless of course you happened to be a musician. In which case you would arrive at the young lady's home in a beat-up van, the engine of which sounded terminally ill. You would normally be wearing jeans, saving the fancy stuff for on stage, help the girl into the back of the van with the gear and the other girlfriends, and tell her parents that, providing the van made it to and fro' the gig, she would probably be home at about three in the morning. Ah me, happy days!

The biographies that follow concern some of Exeter and East Devon's most popular outfits. Of a certainty there are dozens more, and the selection of bands has not been easy. It does, however, leave the matter open-ended, and perhaps there will be a second volume covering this area; we'll see.

It is my sincere hope that the book rekindles some happy memories for the musicians who gave so much pleasure to so many people, and to the recipients of their labours.

Barry Sowden
2003

Barry Sowden

The Groups

PART ONE

The Bluesounds at Torquay
Town Hall

The Bluesounds

In the four short years from conception of The Bluesounds to the dissolution of the band, they achieved far more than could realistically have been expected.

Two former members of the very successful Harlequins, Dave Mulvihill and Andy Barnes, founded the group in 1963. Both boys loved to play blues, whereas their former colleagues were dyed-in-the-wool rock and roll enthusiasts. Seeking this change in direction musically, the lads had frequently discussed the possibility of starting a new band that would play their type of music.

Dave Mulvihill, left, and Andy Barnes

Bass player Dave was an organisational wizard and an extrovert, whilst softly spoken Andy was nervous in the extreme, and the complete antithesis of what a lead guitarist is generally perceived as being, i.e. the flash bloke on the end. However, the two teenagers were a perfectly matched combination when performing in front of an audience.

Dave placed an advertisement in the window of Bill Greenhalgh's music shop, proclaiming that auditions would be held in the function room above the Horse and Groom public house in Heavitree, for the purpose of finding a rhythm guitarist and drummer for an exciting new band.

There were several applicants for both vacancies. John Bridges, a nineteen-year-old former pupil of John Stocker School, who lived in Nelson Road and had walked the considerable distance to Heavitree from the St Thomas area of the city, was chosen as the rhythm guitarist. John had grown up with guitarist Colin Drake and singer Alan Bryant, both of whom were well known on the local circuit, and that, according to Dave Mulvihill, was a good enough reference.

John Bridges

Strolling homeward through the city after the audition, John relived the events of the evening. He had been selected from seven or eight applicants, some of who appeared to be far more adept than him, and was now a member of a rock group. He was still deep in thought when he reached his home, which did not go unnoticed by his parents Lillian and Larry.

'Didn't get the job then son,' said Larry matter-of-factly.
'Yes I did,' replied John.
'So what's on your mind then?' asked Lillian.
'Well,' said John, 'if I'm going to be the rhythm guitarist, why did they give me a pair of maracas to shake for the first three numbers?'

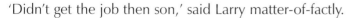

John Bridges and those famous maracas.

Tony Fowler

Listening to Radio Luxembourg on his little transistor later that evening, John clearly detected the unmistakable sound of maracas being shaken by an unseen member of The Rolling Stones. He promptly decided that the hand-held percussion instruments were quite fashionable after all, closed his eyes and went to sleep. A quiet and reserved young man – who had to summon up the courage to enter a High Street shop, much less a dance hall – John had surmounted the first hurdle in his quest to rid himself of the constant feeling of insecurity which beset him.

From the many drummers that attended the audition, four were thought to match the criteria set by Andy and Dave. Unable to conclude which of the short-listed hopefuls was best suited to the band, it was agreed that a full practice with each of the possibles would resolve the matter. Within a few weeks the list had been trimmed by 75 per cent. The surviving runner in the Barnes-Mulvihill 'Find a Drummer Handicap Chase' was Tony Fowler, a fairly steady dance band drummer, who, at thirty years old, was 'getting on a bit', but nevertheless, was a very nice guy with definite potential. Tony was contacted and invited to join The Bluesounds, that being Dave's proposal as to the band's identity, on a permanent basis. To the relief of Dave, Andy, and John, Tony accepted the offer after giving the matter due consideration.

At rehearsals, which took place at Wheatons Social Club in Fore Street, the three youngsters found 'the old man' a pleasure to be with. Any song or tune which required a tempo other than strict ballroom was greeted by Tony with a pseudo-agonised groan, 'I can't play that!'

Of course Tony could play it – but derived tremendous satisfaction from watching bass player Dave thoughtfully demonstrating how it should be done. Dave recollects that he was always impressed with the speed at which Tony 'picked things up', and never realised that Tony was merely 'winding him up'.

As a player manager, Dave Mulvihill was unrivalled. As Andy Barnes put it, 'He could sell fleas to a dog's home.' Testimonies to The Bluesounds' talent were to be seen in shop windows, and the boys were often featured in the local press.

One of The Bluesounds' early gigs was at the club in which they rehearsed, and of which Dave was a member, as an employee of Wheatons. A visitor to the club on this occasion was the Entertainments Secretary of the Student's Guild at Exeter University who liked what he heard, and made a mental note of the band's name and contact address.

John Bridges was becoming accustomed to other musicians giving him a cheery wave and stopping for a natter, all of which was doing his hitherto non-existent confidence a power of good. Tony demonstrated his affection for, and loyalty to, the band when – much to the annoyance of his wife Mary – he traded in his beloved old Standard motor car and bought a van. The verbal reaction of the other Bluesounds to this news, would suggest to the unenlightened that it was only a matter of time before Tony's name appeared in the New Year's Honours List.

A letter from Lionel Digby, the proprietor of LMD Entertainments in Torquay, confirming his interest in The Bluesounds, was to the boys akin to getting eight draws on the treble chance. Certainly one of, if not the largest agency in the South West, LMD solely represented many of the area's top acts including Gary Kane and the Tornadoes, The Mustangs, Mel Fear and The Fantastic Phantoms, The Starfires and The Stringbeats.

Bluesounds fan club letter

Tony Fowler in particular had good reason to remember the first booking received from Lionel. Following an excellent performance to a full house at Torquay Town Hall, the boys were approached by two young women who wanted to start a Bluesounds Fan Club. The girls, Caroline Knott and Celia Knowling, produced pens and paper and proceeded to interview the four highly chuffed musicians.

Names, addresses, dates of birth, likes and dislikes, colour of hair and eyes were all faithfully recorded, and later set out in a fan letter, which was sent to Dave, reproduced by his employer, and the copies despatched to the girls' homes in Torquay, for distribution to all the group's fans. On top of the world, the happy chappies completed the post-gig dismantling of their gear, and carried the first few items out to the van – only to find that it had been 'lovingly vandalised'.

The little Dormobile was covered in graffiti. 'We love you Dave; I love Andy; John is Fab; and Tony is sexy'. These, together with several Torquay telephone numbers, had been daubed on the front, sides, and rear of the van in high-gloss lipstick.

'Oh Hell!' said Tony. 'Mary will go absolutely berserk when she sees this lot.' 'Bit late to do anything about it tonight,' said Dave, trying to memorise two or three telephone numbers.

Early the next morning Dave, Andy and John reported to Tony's house to try to separate the lipstick from the original paintwork. Many buckets of water and gallons of detergent later, the lipstick clung stubbornly. Tony, a fitter by trade, called in a few favours and the van was given a complete respray. Unbelievably, the offending lipstick was still faintly visible after its visit to the spray shop.

Although the majority of The Bluesounds' engagements were in the Exeter and Torquay areas, their appearances were not wholly confined to Devon. A booking at the Winter Gardens in Penzance, Cornwall, turned into a nightmare. The band had entertained the members of the local Chamber of Commerce and played supremely well. At well past midnight, loaded up and readying themselves for the journey back to Exeter, the boys were suddenly surrounded by uniformed policemen.

A tobacconist's shop adjacent to the Winter Gardens had been robbed earlier in the evening, and the owner, who had enjoyed a pleasant evening dancing to a band called The Bluesounds, had just discovered the theft. The lads were escorted to Penzance police station, vehemently protesting their innocence, and were held for at least an hour until the shopkeeper was able to confirm their whereabouts at the time the robbery was thought to have taken place. The duty sergeant was still unconvinced that the four long-haired yobs were not in some way connected to the theft, and insisted that they be escorted to the Devon/Cornwall border.

On reaching the county border near Launceston, the Panda car overtook the van and signalled it to stop. Andy Barnes, who had been waiting for an opportunity to answer the call of nature, slipped silently through the rear door of the van, closing the door behind him. Crouching low, he noiselessly hastened to a gateway some 10 yards back down the road. The policeman, who had merely wanted to apologise for any inconvenience caused, got back in his car and drove off, Tony following in his wake with radio blaring. Thirty minutes later, a cold and irate lead guitarist was retrieved, and the homeward journey completed without further incident or speech, other than the occasional snigger from Dave Mulvihill.

During the next two years, The Bluesounds were billed with many top professional acts such as Sounds Incorporated, The Animals, Brian Poole and the Tremeloes, and The Moody Blues. Taking part in a three-band extravaganza at the University of Exeter with Gary Kane and the Tornadoes, and The Who, the boys were more than a little smug when the audience displayed their preference for the local groups, by walking out of the hall during Roger Daltrey's opening number.

The Bluesounds were the first outfit to play at St George's Hall, Exeter, and well remember it. The heavy, metal-ribbed curtains, which glided effortlessly across the forward section of the imposing stage to herald an interval, broke the glass on a badly sited fire alarm which activated the sprinkler system, and pandemonium ensued.

In 1967 Andy Barnes started his own hairdressing business, and found the obligatory Saturday opening of the shop, followed by a gig that more often than not meant travelling many miles, tiring in the extreme. John Bridges too was suffering from terminal tedium, and had taken solace from 'depping' with The Harlequins, and The Secrets. Discussing their respective problems with Dave Mulvihill and drummer Tony Fowler, Andy and John were relieved to find that their colleagues were both sympathetic and understanding. The Bluesounds could not have broken up more amicably.

Dave said that he would probably try to form another band, and Tony philosophically declared that it would make a refreshing change to be able to book a holiday for himself and his family without first consulting his personal gig guide.

The Codiaks and The Future Impressions

Part of an interview between the author and drummer/bass guitarist Peter Evans.

Barry: 'Thanks for giving up your time to talk to me Pete, I think it vitally important that the biography be accurate, don't you?'

Pete: 'Er, well yes, would you like a cup of tea?'

Barry: 'That would be nice… milk no sugar ta, perhaps we can talk while you're brewing it?'

Pete: 'OK.'

Barry: 'So tell me, where did the name The Codiaks come from?'

Pete: 'That's an easy one, it was Robin's idea – or was it Graham's? It might have been mine. No, I'm positive it was Rob; it *was* a long time ago.'

Barry: 'I'll check with him then shall I?'

Pete: 'Good idea. Rob's bound to remember. He was a brilliant musician – did all his own arrangements you know.'

Barry: 'So I understand – Dave Mulvihill speaks very highly of him.'

Pete: 'Dave Mulvihill – I played golf with him a while ago, how is he?'

Barry: 'I think he's extremely busy, it took me quite a long time to pin him down for a chat.'

Pete: 'Yeah that's Dave, always on the go. Here's your tea … now where were we?'

Barry: 'I was asking who came up with the name Codiaks.'

Pete: 'Well, I'm fairly sure it was Robin Phillips, how's your tea?'

Barry: 'Fine thanks, you not having one?'

Pete: 'No, I don't think it would sit too well – I arranged to meet a customer in the Cowick Barton at lunchtime and a few of my mates happened to be there. You know how it is, a dead sensible couple of pints of Guinness and all of a sudden you're into a sesh; if I hadn't come home when I did, I'd still be there. God I feel sleepy … what were you asking about Dave?'

Barry: 'Dave?…'

Guitarist Robin Phillips did indeed christen the group The Codiaks. Teenager Robin, together with Graham Daniel and of course Peter Evans, were members of the youth club held in St Lawrence Church Hall at Hill Barton, between Pinhoe and Exeter. Robin and Graham owned acoustic guitars and could play one or two Shadows numbers, Graham picking out the melody, and Robin playing most of the chords. At fifteen years of age, Peter, an apprenticed electrician with Howard, Woodland & Stephens based in Sidwell Street, Exeter, was younger than his two friends. He was, however, able to join in the fun when he used some of his weekly wage of £2.15s.0d (£2.75) to purchase a pair of drumsticks – which were then used to 'play' the guitar cases belonging to his pals.

'Hey Mr Tambourine Man'…
Robin Phillips

'Live' at St Lawrence church hall: (L–R) Graham Daniel, Pete Evans, Alan Hart, Robin Phillips

Three months of rehearsal in the garage adjoining Robin's parents' house, where Peter had a vast array of items to hit, including the wheel trims on the Phillips' family car, convinced the trio that they were going to make it to the very top.

These fantasies were reinforced by the recruitment of Alan Hart. Alan, a friend of Peter's from their days at Vincent Thompson School, joined The Codiaks as the bass guitarist, and gave the line-up a traditional look, with the obvious exception of a drum-kit. This was rectified with a total withdrawal from Peter's Post Office Savings Account, topped up with a loan from Mr Evans Snr, and a subsequent Saturday morning visit to Bill Greenhalgh's.

The Codiaks' first public appearance was at the St Lawrence Youth Club. Peter actually appeared there five times; unable to make satisfactory logistical arrangements (his mum and dad had thoughtlessly gone shopping), he made four journeys on foot from Birchy Barton Hill, carrying his recently acquired drums to the venue for the band's debut performance.

The performance proved surprising, not only to the four young members of the band whose efforts were applauded, but for the audience. They might have been justified in expecting more than eight numbers from the lads, regardless of how well they were played, especially when the second half of the evening featured the same eight tunes as the first.

Nevertheless, the boys had benefited from the experience, and had taken heart from the fact that the audience had neither heckled, nor thrown anything at them. The Codiaks generally agreed that the purchase of a PA system and additional amplification was of paramount importance. Robin and Graham had built their own electric guitars and the meagre 30-watt-output of the single amplifier used to 'power' both instruments was totally inadequate.

Is that Brian Jones on the left?

A pair of mail-order Heathkit 50-watt-output 'self-build' amplifiers, assembled by some enterprising students from St Loye's College under the watchful eye of a teacher who happened to be a friend of Graham Daniel, were used for PA and for the rhythm guitar. Robin sang the vocals, of which very few were needed to double the band's repertoire, into a microphone that had been supplied with an antiquated reel-to-reel tape recorder. In the absence of a stand, the microphone was suspended from the light fitting in the lounge of Peter's long-suffering parents' house. Mum and Dad Evans had been afforded the dubious honour of witnessing the band's very first vocal – a foot-tapping, neighbour-startling version of The Beatles' 'I Saw Her Standing There'.

In the following months, as finances improved, the boys invested in a Reslo ribbon microphone and, later still, another microphone with the brand-name Grampian, both of which had been designed and advertised as being eminently suitable for both singing, and public address.

During the next two years, The Codiaks' weekly rehearsal, coupled with the occasional booking at a local youth club or village hall and Robin Phillip's talent for arrangement, turned the band into a pleasant-sounding, well-drilled outfit. Pete Evan's enthusiasm was fired by three major factors. Firstly, he loved the music that he and his friends were playing. Secondly, he had recently taken delivery of a brand-new kit of Premier drums, complete with all the accessories. The drums were purchased from Bill Greenhalgh's using his in-house 'play-as-you-pay' system, without which many musicians throughout the South West would never have possessed their own instrument(s). The third and final reason for Peter's drive and determination resulted from a visit to the Athena Club to listen to The Bluesounds. One of Exeter's top bands of the moment and a personal favourite of Peter's. The Bluesounds' performances never failed to impress him – as did the sight of band leader Dave Mulvihill doling out a handful of dog-eared pound notes to his colleagues after the gig.

The sun's a bit bright today innit? (L–R) Pete Evans, Dave Crowden, Denis White, Robin Phillips

1965 was a year of transformation for The Codiaks in that founder member Graham Daniel and bass guitarist Alan Hart left to pursue other interests, their places being taken by rhythm guitarist Denis White and bassist Dave Crowden, and the group's musical preference changed from rock and roll to rhythm and blues. The Spencer Davis Group was the root cause of this diversification. Appearing at the America Hall in Pinhoe as part of a national tour to promote their first album, the outfit from Birmingham (although Spencer himself was born in Swansea, South Wales) emphasised the yawning chasm that exists between the amateur and the professional.

Together with seventeen-year-old vocalist and keyboard player Steve Winwood, around whom the group was doubtless focused, guitarist/vocalist Spencer Davis, drummer Peter York, and bass guitarist Mervyn 'Muff' Winwood the older brother of Steve, turned in a mind-blowing performance which had the audience screaming for more. Standing amongst the huge crowd, the four members of The Codiaks cheered and applauded right along with them. Peter recalls that he felt sorry for the supporting act that evening. The Tycoons – Pete Starkey, Terry Stevens, Dave Newcombe, Steve Bradley and Mike Brown-King – were a polished and well-rehearsed outfit who acquitted themselves wonderfully well, but they too seemed somewhat overawed by the chart-topping lads from the Midlands.

A copy of the Spencer Davis debut album was ordered by Pete Evans, and he, Robin, Denis and Dave set about the task of learning the melody and lyrics of every track. Slowly but surely the boys changed their playing style, Robin Phillips striving to ensure with his skilful arrangements that not only would any audience recognise the number, they would in the future associate it with The Codiaks as well as Spencer Davis. New releases by groups such as The Who and The Small Faces were rehearsed and played in the same week, and the boys' reputation as a 'mod' band grew. The parka-wearing, scooter-riding fraternity followed The Codiaks across the county, and it was not unusual to see 50-odd Lambrettas and Vespas parked outside a dance hall when the boys were appearing there.

DANCES PARTIES SHOWS

The

CODIAKS

BEAT-GROUP

Manager: J. Orton 32, Raleigh Road,
(Johnny Cordell) Exeter.
Tel. 59827

Wanna book The Codiaks?

Signed by both LMD and Starline Entertainments, the lads ventured into all four corners of Devon with the occasional gig in Cornwall. They became much in demand as a support act, appearing with The Kinks, Dave Berry, Wee Willy Harris, Neil Christian, Simon Dupree, The Equals and many other big names. The Codiaks were also booked to entertain the England's victorious World Cup football squad, at the Ace of Clubs in Plymouth's Union Street. After an incredible night, the boys headed back to Exeter and a very welcome fry-up at 'Dirty Dot's café' in Cowick Street. They left just as people with 'real jobs' were setting off to work, and then remembered that they had 'real jobs' themselves.

When Denis decided that he no longer 'got a buzz' from playing and departed, Robin, Dave and Peter continued as a trio for a short period. Dave, for reasons best known to him, followed suit. Robin and Peter discussed the possibility of recruiting replacements but concurred that it might be nice to try something different, perhaps by joining another band. It proved to be the case. Robin linked up with superb saxophonist Ray Beavis, the Darlison brothers, Tony Benellick and Terry Denning, former drummer of both The Nightlights and Starfires, in a band called The In-Sect, prior to becoming a prize catch for the Hip Hooray Good Times Band.

The best of brass: (L–R) Pauline Pring, Alan Hart, Roy Bradford

Pete Evans resolved to take time out and catch up with the million and one things that he had meant to do during the past four years and never got around to doing. These praiseworthy thoughts were uppermost in his mind for at least a month before the urge to take the stage once again prevailed. His girlfriend Pauline Pring, from a brass-banding family, and an extremely competent trumpet player having played with Topsham Silver Band for several years, was persuaded to join the brass section of what Peter envisaged as being a fairly large soul band.

Her sister Janet was inveigled into becoming the outfit's drummer on the strength of Pete's offer to teach her to play. True to his word, Peter did provide the necessary instruction, and promptly sold her his drum-kit, having decided that he would like to become a bass player. Two former members of The Codiaks, Denis White and Alan Hart, were contacted along with Mike Brailey, Roy Bradford, Tony Benellick, Alan Curtis, Roger Richards, Ray Beavis and Derek Holmes. From these nine musicians – some in a permanent capacity while others 'depped' – together with Pauline, Janet and Peter, sprang Exeter's latest and certainly biggest band, Future Impressions. The band was however, short-lived. The cost of running and hiring a ten-piece proved to be beyond local budgets.

Drumming up a storm, Janet Pring

Happily, the majority of the musicians involved with Future Impressions joined other bands, Ray Beavis probably claiming the most success by becoming a member of the Hip Hooray GT Band. Pauline and Peter initially joined an outfit called Dance Scene, although Peter left soon after. Prior to finally consigning his beloved Fender Precision bass guitar to a far corner of the broom cupboard, Peter played with Son-Set, Nice & Easy, Looking Glass, The Mike Johnson Trio, The Chris Winter Band and The River Set.

'Phew, it was a busy old time wasn't it Pete; any chance of another cup of tea?'

Alan Hart, left, and Denis White

If music be the food of love – why did I join the Catering Corps?

Formerly a chef at the Burlington restaurant and the Queen's Hotel in Exeter, John Greenslade followed in the footsteps of his father, Captain Frank Greenslade, and joined the Army. After his basic training at the Army Catering Corps depot in Aldershot, John was posted, via St Omar barracks and the successful completion of several other courses, to Ashchurch near Tewkesbury, in Gloucestershire.

A diligent soldier, John quickly began to ascend the non-commissioned ladder, rising from lance-corporal, then corporal, to acting-sergeant. The stripes denoting these positions, however, appeared to spend as much time in the top drawer of the quartermaster's desk as they did adorning Private, Lance-Corporal, or Corporal Greenslade's upper arms. He was demoted almost as often as he was promoted. This was wholly due to John's fervent love of his native West Country – and in particular Exeter. 'Foreigners' (anywhere north of Taunton) continually mimicking the Devonian accent, referring to swede-bashers, milking smocks and wellies, were forcibly reminded that John's other great passion was boxing.

'You wouldn't speak to me like that if you weren't wearing those stripes' was the sullen reply to a ticking-off by Lance-Corporal, Corporal, or Acting-Sergeant Greenslade. Removing his jacket, John would invariably rise to the challenge, prove the mickey-taker wrong, and duly report to the commanding officer the following day to have his stripes officially removed. Thankfully, this did not happen often enough to affect John 'what rank am I today?' Greenslade's ranking as a popular member of the billet.

One of his pals, a lad called Rankin, was a self-taught guitarist who enjoyed nothing better than belting out skiffle numbers when he could. When in 1958 John's wife June bought him a steel-strung flat-top guitar as a birthday present, John returned to the barracks after his weekend leave, immediately sought out Private Rankin, and requested that he be shown a few chords.

Twelve months later, John was posted back to his beloved Exeter. Stationed first at Higher, then Wyvern Barracks, his life became more agreeable. On a visit to the Mint Methodist Youth Club the Rankin-trained guitarist asked David Gray, the leader of a skiffle group called Group Two which was playing that evening, if he could sit in. After listening to John play a tune which contained several ninth and diminished chords, Mr Gray, who presumably had never seen or heard these chords before, refused his request on the grounds that John couldn't play the instrument properly.

Shortly after this rebuff John met someone who was to be a lifelong friend, Percy Turner. A plumber by trade, Exeter-born Percy, like John Greenslade, had an all-consuming interest in sound recording and worked for the BBC on a sub-contract basis. A superlative guitarist, he had played with the skiffle group that subsequently evolved into The Tornadoes.

That a band would be formed was inevitable, and in the early 60s the addition of bass-playing civil servant John Fewings and drummer Alan Pearson – a motor mechanic specialising in diesel engines – to the duo of Greenslade and Turner, resulted in Exeter's newest outfit, The Corvettes.

Percy came up with the name Corvettes, and it was his amazing guitar skills combined with John's extensive knowledge of chord shapes, allied to a better-than-average bass player and a competent drummer, that set the band on the road to success almost from the outset. Rehearsals were largely unnecessary. Percy would hear the first few lines of a popular melody, inform John G. and John F. of the key in which he wished to play, count in the band and simply play it.

There were occasions when the rhythm section had great difficulty in keeping up. Percy had heard a tune called 'Orange Blossom Special', an extremely lively piece which many country & western acts had recorded over the years. Studio trickery was often used when recording this particular tune. The artiste would play the number at a slow speed, the tape would be sped up during the playback, and the resulting high-speed track duplicated and used as the master copy.

The Corvettes with Kay Scott

This ingenious con meant that the majority of mere mortal guitarists found it impossible to play as per the record, unless, of course, the guitarist in question happened to be 'warp-speed' Perc. John Greenslade fondly recalls an enthusiastic audience in a packed Exeter Civic Hall standing open-mouthed as Percy played the tune live, and the thunderous applause when he had finished. 'Unbelievable,' says John, 'absolutely unbelievable!'

To say that The Corvettes was a good band, is rather like saying that the Sultan of Brunei has got a few bob. As a purely instrumental rock outfit they were peerless. But it was this unilateral style that prompted the quartet to advertise for a vocalist which resulted in the addition of Kay Benellick. Adopting the stage name of Kay Scott, she fronted The Corvettes for about eighteen months and married drummer Alan Pearson, but for reasons unknown both left the band in 1961. Their replacements were vocalist Tony Osborne, and teenage drummer Dave Smale.

Born in Coventry, moving to Exeter as a young boy, Tony Osborne joined Her Majesty's Royal Electrical and Mechanical Engineers in 1955. A devotee of the big-band sounds, Tony's influences were Ted Heath, Dickie Valentine and Matt Munro. Posted to the Far East, Tony bought a cheap Spanish guitar and was taught to play the obligatory four-chord sequence in the key of C by a mucker (army colleague) and whiled away many a long hour strumming and singing.

Tony enjoyed his spell in Hong Kong, but was a trifle peeved when one of his heroes, Matt Munro, arrived to perform a series of BFPO (British Forces Posted Overseas) concerts for the troops, on the very day that he (Tony) was returning to the UK. Demobbed at the end of 1958, back in Exeter and searching for some entertainment, Tony went to a dance at the Civic Hall to listen to The Corvettes. Introducing himself to the lads during the break, he briefly expounded his musical experience to date and was asked to attend the next rehearsal. Tony got the job and fronted The Corvettes until 1964.

Tony Osborne outside the ABC Cinema. On the posters in the windows Helen Shapiro and Eden Kane

Drummer Dave Smale detested music at school. Frankly, Mr Victor Webber, the music teacher at Ladysmith Secondary Modern, despaired. David was interested only in sport, especially football and table tennis at which he excelled, representing his school in both. It was usual for Dave and his pal Jeff Folland to train for table tennis competitions at the City Mission Youth Club, an annexe of Bradley Rowe School used also as the headquarters of the Boys' Brigade. Intensive practice sessions were under way to attain the prestigious National Association of Boys Clubs award, and the two fourteen-year-olds had special permission to remain in the club after everyone had gone home, lock up, and return the key to the caretaker.

One evening, what could be described as mild cacophony broke Dave and Jeff's concentration. (That's not quite how Dave referred to it!) Looking out of the window they saw the Boys' Brigade Band appear, led by a gentleman named 'Skip' Vidgon. With bugles blaring and drums rattling the band marked time outside of the club until Skip ordered, 'Band halt, Band dismissed'. The Brigade entered the building, stowed their instruments away and went home – forgetting to lock up the cupboard.

Moments later, Jeff was vainly striving to obtain some sort of sound from a bugle, and Dave was happily bashing away on a snare drum. The impromptu jam session ended as quickly as it had started. Jeff, with all thoughts of emulating Eddie Calvert (the man with the golden trumpet) forgotten, returned the bugle to its rightful place, as did Dave with the drum set, and the boys continued their game of table tennis.

The following year, Jeff and Dave represented Ladysmith School in the inter-schools sports competition held at the County ground, and both won their respective events. Dave also fell hopelessly in love. The blissfully unaware recipient of Dave's first schoolboy crush was called Diane Kelland who was there with her friend Jean Rank, representing St Thomas's School for Girls. But she was responsible, albeit indirectly, for Dave becoming a drummer. A school friend, Tony Haggett, told Dave that he was going to a dance at the Women's Institute in Ide Lane on the forthcoming Saturday night, and the girls would probably be there.

On the night of the dance, Dave and Tony cycled to Ide Lane. Their bicycles were 'parked' behind the hedge (it wasn't cool to arrive with neither car nor motorcycle), the boys tendered their 2s.6d. (12.5p) admission fee and went in. Dave realised within minutes that the girl of his dreams was not there. Despondent, he bought an orange squash and mingled for a while. The band called an intermission and the little hall emptied.

Five minutes later, in the saloon bar of The New Inn public house with a pint of bitter that had been bought for him by one of the bigger boys, Dave was surprised to see the drummer of the skiffle group that had been playing at Ide Lane earlier, suddenly stagger and fall down. It was apparently Wally Clark's birthday and he was a popular chap. Guitarist and group leader Roger Flood gave out an impassioned plea, 'Is there a drummer in the house?'

The Nightlights: (L–R) Ian Scanes, Dave Parsons, Dave Gray, Dave Smale, out of shot left, Roger Cavill

Front cover of BMG programme

Corvettes entry in rhythm and blues section (number 14)

'My mate can play,' shouted Tony Haggett, pointing at Dave. Introducing himself, the group leader said, 'Four beats to the bar, you can't go wrong.' Convinced that Roger was speaking fluent gibberish Dave returned to the dance hall, sat behind the sparkly drum-kit and repeated the performance he had given many months earlier on the Boys' Brigade side drum. Dave lost count of the number of boys and girls who congratulated him after the dance, and his musical career had begun.

The months flew by. Dave left school and although his ambition had been to become a motor mechanic, started work as a painter and decorator with a building firm, owned by Arthur Flood. By chance, Arthur was the father of Roger Flood, the guitarist with the skiffle group who had played at the Women's Institute in Ide Lane.

He was invited to become the drummer of local band Ricky and The Nightlights – providing, of course, that he bought a drum-kit. As so often happens, it was mum to the rescue. An unsecured loan of £13 enabled him to buy a second-hand snare drum complete with stand, a pair of drumsticks, and a bass drum with a foot pedal 'thrown-in', by who else but kind-hearted Bill Greenhalgh.

The Nightlights – vocalist Roger 'Ricky' Cavill, lead guitarist Dave Gray (later replaced by Tiverton's Paul Midgeley), guitarist and bass player Dave Parsons, ex Cathedral School pupil and saxophonist Ian Scanes (affectionately nicknamed Fred) and drummer Dave Smale – became Danny and the Nightlights shortly after Dave's arrival, when Roger 'Ricky' Cavill decided that the name Danny sounded better.

Having no transport, and much to the amusement of some passengers and the annoyance of others, Dave got his drums to gigs by Corporation bus. This unsatisfactory state of affairs was sorted when he was granted permission to store them at the Mint Methodist Youth Club where the band regularly played. Countless hours of practice reaped dividends. Dave developed a powerful style and technique, which was the envy of many a counterpart, and it was perhaps inevitable that this brilliance would attract the attention of other outfits.

Contest No. 25. "RHYTHM & BLUES" for Boosey & Hawkes "Fernandos" Jumbo Guitar.

1. Wes Minster Five	8. Blueologists	16. Desmond Browne
2. Stella Lennox	9. Gerry Oswald	17. Gloria Hale
3. Stephanie Kayne	10. Vilma Ross	18. Bill Edwards
4. Ray Burt	11. The Fellow Men	19. The Westerners
5. Patricia	12. Errol Rosemund	20. D. Brown
6. Jay Lopaka & the Coral Islanders	13. Victor Vincent	21. Joanne Price
7. John Dean	14. Corvettes Rhythm Group	22. Vean & Jean
	15. Laverne Brown	23. B. E. Chaplin

Contest No. 26. "ROCK GROUPS" for "Vox" Guitar and Watkins "Copicat" Unit.

1. Les Andrews Four	6. The Escalators	11. Jenny Oakland and her Western Swingers
2. The Zircons	7. The Rebels	
3. The Deltones	8. The Gremlins	12. Desmond Browne
4. The Cousins	9. The Hellcats	13. The Runners
5. Ricky Ford & the Crossfires	10. Western Swingers	14. The Zeros

The Corvettes with The Beatles

Corvettes rhythm guitarist John Greenslade had followed Dave's career with interest and when Alan Pearson left, sent manager Dick Miller to offer him the position. His acceptance took The Corvettes into the top flight of the semi-professional music scene, playing both locally, and throughout Devon, Cornwall and Somerset, as the band's popularity soared. Signed by trad jazz legend Acker Bilk to his Bilk Marketing Company in December 1962, the boys were honoured to be the South West's sole representatives at the 26th Musical Festival and Rally, organised by the British Federation of Banjoists, Mandolinists and Guitarists and held in London's St Pancras Town Hall on Saturday 18 May 1963. An astounding performance on the night merited the panel of judges' decision to declare The Corvettes the third-best amateur rock outfit in England!

'Chiefy' Pasternack, stage manager of the ABC Cinema in Exeter, whose job included the setting-up of tours for chart-toppers from both sides of the Atlantic, became a good friend to The Corvettes, allowing them not only to

Rocking at the Athena Club: Sandra Turner, June Greenslade and Lillian Osborne

use the cinema for rehearsals, but also to join the tours as a support act. The Beatles had recently reached the top of the Hit Parade (the Charts) with a song called 'Love Me Do' and were booked to appear at the ABC. The Corvettes were invited by Chiefy to meet the Fab Four and watch from the wings.

The evening was memorable. Dave Smale, who had 'teamed-up' with Ringo Starr, introduced him to a unique new sound, obtained by removing the chain and plug from the wash-basin in the dressing room and draping it over a crash cymbal. John Greenslade and George Harrison, meanwhile, were bawled out and banished to the fire escape for smoking backstage. After The Beatles' performance, Tony Osborne, listening to Paul McCartney rehearsing a new song called 'Please, Please Me' on the 'house piano', joined Paul in singing the first verse.

The Corvettes were booked to appear on the opening night of the Athena Club as a showcase. The next day, manager Dick Miller called the lads together and told them that they were to be a part of the ABC programme, and would be touring with all the top acts. But Perc Turner, who had adopted the stage name Tony Turner, decided that he could not commit himself on a professional basis and left the band.

Exeter-based guitarist Ray Hill, among many others, was auditioned for the vacancy that Tony Turner had created, but The Corvettes were a spent force. John Fewings, taken into hospital with severe influenza that developed complications, tragically passed away before he could sample the life of a professional musician. Bass player Len Simpson filled in as a temporary measure until the arrival of Jersey-born bass guitarist Norman Vautier, the brother in-law of Dave Smale.

Having agreed that The Corvettes could never hope to be the slick outfit they had once been, John Greenslade, Tony Osborne, Norman Vautier, and Dave Smale called it a day. John Greenslade joined Gary Kane's Tornadoes; Tony Osborne took the stage name of Mark Shannon and founded a band called The Sunsets with Ray Hill, Tommy Gibson, Len Simpson and Robin Hatherley; Norman Vautier returned to Jersey; and Dave Smale became an extremely busy freelance.

Mark Shannon and the Sunsets: (L–R) Tommy Gibson, Robin Hatherley, Ray Hill, Len Simpson, Tony Osborne

The Cougars

Towards the end of 1959 at Hele School in Exeter, Mike Lloyd bought an old flat-top guitar and started strumming away at home, attempting to sound like the stars of the day, notably Lonnie Donegan and a relatively new guy on the block, Cliff Richard.

The following week, at school, he was talking to Trevor Inch who had bought a guitar and wanted to learn a few chords. The two got together and found that Trevor had an old valve radio at his house, into the back of which a guitar could be plugged. All that was needed was a pick-up, which was bought from Bill Greenhalgh for £1.10s.6d.

The nucleus of a new band, which it had been agreed was going to sound exactly like instrumental group The Shadows, was formed. Additional recruits were Richard Townsend from Whimple near Exeter, who owned a snare drum and small cymbal (he also threatened to buy some drumsticks as well), and another pupil at Hele's, Ricky Angus. Ricky kindly offered to play bass, totally unfazed by the fact that he neither possessed nor could play the instrument.

Still at school, Mike Lloyd had a Saturday-morning job at Bill Greenhalgh's and had noticed a rather nice Hofner Senator guitar which had a built-in pick-up, and even had controls. Whilst it looked good, the finger action was not all that special, and being fitted with tape-wound strings, the guitar sounded awful. Nevertheless, a deal was arranged with Bill and he bought it for £15. Ricky bought a Hofner similar to Mike's, and Trevor acquired a slightly cheaper model, the 'Club 40'. The quest for that Shadows' trembling sound continued, and Mike bought a Supersound tremolo unit for the Hofner. It looked good and promised to sound great but had the disconcerting property of making the guitar go out of tune. Mike just hoped

Mike Lloyd, at home with his flat-top

Robert E Lee and the Confederates: Behind (L–R), Mike Lloyd, Trevor Inch, Ricky Angus. Front, Richard Townsend

that before long his competence would improve enough to put the band into the top flight, and he would be able to afford the equipment he so longed to own. Meanwhile, Richard had been given a bass drum and was scouring the second-hand shops for a 'high hat'.

Roger Langford-Thomas, another pupil at Hele's, suggested that he join as vocalist, and the band, known as Robert E Lee and the Confederates, was 'launched'. Playing on Saturday mornings at the Gaumont cinema in North Street, Exeter, before the first picture show of the day brought them other bookings. Whilst the venues were invariably local youth clubs, the band would play in any room or hall where the stage or playing area was adjacent to a five-amp socket – they didn't possess an extension lead!

Now we've got a singer! Standing, second-right, Roger Langford-Thomas.

Ricky Angus bought himself a Slender bass guitar, Mike part-exchanged his pretty (but an absolute nightmare to play) Hofner for a Broadway Guyatone, and Trevor bought a Watkins Dominator amp. Richard had found a high hat and the boys were given an old microphone, but still more changes were on the way.

On Friday nights, the band would normally be found performing at the Clifton Hill Club. The club, situated in the cellars of a large house in Clifton Hill, Exeter (not surprisingly the origin of its name), owned by the parents of school friend Dave Ross, would on busy evenings host 70 or 80 enthusiastic teenagers.

One night, John Ffoulkes, who was a regular visitor to the cellar and had noticed that the band was without its singer, asked if he could sing. Looking and sounding remarkably like Cliff Richard, he became the outfit's permanent vocalist, Roger having recently decided to leave. With a change of singer, and additional equipment – a Fenton Weil Reverberation unit had been added and Mike had bought a Hofner V3 solid-bodied guitar – it seemed to the boys that it was an appropriate moment to change the name of the band, and thus The Cougars were born.

Weekly rehearsals, also held at the Clifton Club, eventually resulted in a comprehensive library of both instrumentals and vocals. Talented lead guitarist Mike Lloyd appeared to experience little difficulty in producing the correct

The Cougars at the Clifton Club: (L–R) Richard Townsend, Ricky Angus, Mike Lloyd, Trevor Inch

notation to many quite often tricky tunes, by the John Barry Seven, Duane Eddy etc., and John Ffoulkes's voice was ideally suited to cover numbers by Adam Faith, Billy Fury and Eddie Cochran.

News of the Cougars' formation and ability reached the ears of Bill Sprague, who lived in Exeter and promoted dances at the city's Civic Hall, the Victory Hall in Broadclyst, and the Town Hall in Crediton, in addition to several youth clubs in the area. Bill made a point of listening to the band playing live at the Clifton Club – fast becoming the city's answer to the Cavern Club in Liverpool – and liked what he had heard.

The band was placed at the head of Bill's booking list and became busy, fast! With an abundance of engagements and stage wear – Trevor Inch's mum had kindly 'run-up' a dressy jacket for each of them – the group lacked for nothing except transport. All being seventeen, none of the teenagers could drive so the equipment from necessity was conveyed to each function by double-decker bus.

This unsatisfactory situation was resolved by someone who became a good friend to The Cougars, a Mr Share, verger at Whipton church, next door to which was the youth club. Talking to the lads after a successful dance at the youth club, Mr Share remarked that he had not seen the 'band wagon' parked outside. When he learned that this was usually the local bus, he kindly offered the use of both himself and his vehicle, a Ford Classic, for all future engagements.

Trevor had left school to train as an apprentice electrician and acquired a BSA Bantam motorbike to speed him from job to job, which after passing his test, was superseded by a 250cc machine. Riding through Exeter, and in no particular hurry, Trevor was in collision with a motor car, catapulted from his machine and thrown over the car head first into the side of a bus. As a result of severe cranial injuries, the luckless lad would be ruled out of any band activity for many months.

The other members – John, Mike, Ricky and Richard – themselves badly traumatised by the accident, decided in deference to Trevor that they would not look for another rhythm guitarist and The Cougars disbanded.

For a while Mike Lloyd 'depped' with local bands The Harlequins and Danny and the Nightlights in addition to providing 'sickness cover' for John 'Ginger' Walker – the lead guitarist of Tiverton's Kenny and the Starfires – before joining Sounds Unlimited on a permanent basis. John Ffoulkes became the front man with Gary Whitehead's Harlequins, and Richard Townsend joined a jazz band. The Cougars would never return, or be heard again.

Or would they...?

In 1986 a reunion of all of the members of Mount Pleasant Youth Club in Exeter was organised at the Countess Wear Motel in Exeter by Steve Phillips, a frequent visitor to the Clifton Hill Club. Mike Lloyd was invited and offered to act as disc jockey for the evening. He decided that, in keeping with the nature of the event, he would spin records from the 1960s (he hadn't played, or owned a guitar since the age of nineteen), but then as an afterthought, wondered if The Cougars could be reborn.

During the next couple of weeks, and with commendable tenacity, Mike managed to track down his former colleagues. Richard Townsend had initially disappeared to deepest Cornwall but had recently relocated to Exeter, and John Ffoulkes had achieved an ambition held since his school days and was now a photographer with the *Express & Echo* newspaper in the city. Sadly, Ricky Angus had died, but when experienced guitarist Mike Emery, who was also on the reunion guest list, expressed his willingness to play bass, Mike rang Steve Phillips and proposed that the entertainment for the evening be provided by The Cougars.

One other pleasant surprise lay in store. Trevor Inch had emigrated to Australia some fifteen years earlier, but had that very week returned to his roots to investigate the possibility of moving back to the UK, and was to stay in Exeter for a few months. He told the delighted Mike Lloyd that he still played the guitar, had swapped his Hofner Club 40 for a Fender Telecaster, and that he would be absolutely delighted to take part in what was sure to be an emotional and enjoyable evening.

The Cougars: back (L–R) Mike Emery, Mike Lloyd; front (L–R) Trevor Inch, Richard Townsend, John Ffoulkes

The Cougars went into serious rehearsal, Mike even buying a Fender Stratocaster although he had to borrow some amplification, and slowly but surely the sounds of the 60s came alive once more. A PA system was arranged (borrowed from another band), as was a lighting rig. The show was starting to take shape.

Over 200 people attended the gala occasion, which was full of familiar faces, nostalgia and tales from the past. The Cougars took the stage for a two-hour stint, playing all of the old favourites and turning back the clock by recreating many of the original sounds, much to the delight of all present.

Following the reunion, the boys were interviewed both by the local press and radio stations, which in turn led to immediate offers of work. Within what they had already decided would be the Cougar's very last week, the band played in rock and roll shows at the Centre Spot at Exeter City Football Ground, the Exeter City Police Club and the Countess Wear Motel. On the last night of the week, The Cougars performed together for the final time at the Crown and Sceptre near the Iron Bridge in Exeter, to a capacity audience.

Trevor Inch did not stay in Exeter, electing instead to return to Australia. Richard Townsend left Exeter for Chulmleigh and Mike Lloyd moved to Bristol. Only John Ffoulkes remained in Exeter to bask in the glory of what was The Cougars.

Four Steps Beyond

When two former members of The Harlequins, Mike Emery and Colin Drake, bumped into each other by chance in a well-known Exeter music emporium in 1964, boredom was the main topic of conversation. Neither of the musicians had taken the stage for almost three weeks. Mike had been the rhythm guitarist with the now-disbanded Secrets, and Colin had occasionally 'depped', happily playing lead or bass guitar as required.

It had to happen of course, but Mike couldn't recall who eventually made the suggestion. However, both left Bill Greenhalgh's shop on Fore Street hill with a sunnier outlook on life. Ex- Mustangs lead guitarist Geoff Cox, vocalist Alan Bryant, and drummer Roger Walker, both of whom had also been members of The Harlequins, were speedily contacted, and joined Mike and Colin in their new band named, unusually for a quintet, Four Steps Beyond.

A minimal number of rehearsals brought the five experienced musicians to a standard thought to be acceptable to themselves, and to the paying public. These practice sessions took place in a barn, on a farm at Dunsford, near Exeter, owned by an obliging farmer called Len.

'Obviously a lover of good music,' commented Mike Emery.

News of the band's formation quickly spread, and offers of work began to pour in. Playing mainly in the Exeter and Torquay areas, the sound of Four Steps Beyond, based mainly on that of The Hollies, was always well received by audiences. Showcased at the '400' Club in Torquay by both Starline and

Four Steps Beyond: (L–R) Mike Emery, Colin Drake, Alan Bryant, Roger Walker, Geoff Cox

The Carousel Club in Copenhagen

LMD agencies, the boys were pleased to be signed by both organisations, and were soon appearing with professional acts like Millie, The Fortunes, and The Hollies, all of who were touring the South West at that time.

The gregarious nature of musicians is sometimes misinterpreted by jealous girlfriends as flirting, or 'chatting up', but it was thanks to Geoff Cox's pleasant nature that Four Steps Beyond became a professional band. Enjoying a drink in a Torquay hostelry on a warm Sunday afternoon, Geoff struck up a conversation with two attractive young women and explained that he was a guitarist. It transpired that the girls were also in the entertainment business, being part of a dance troupe similar to the famous Tiller Girls. Geoff promptly gave them Mike Emery's phone number and laughingly suggested that they put in a good word with their agent when they returned to London.

Three weeks later Mike, who privately thought that Geoff had dreamt the entire episode, was astounded to receive a telephone call from a Vic Sutcliffe. Calling from his office in London, Vic invited the band to attend an interview at his agency's premises in Little Argyle Street, which he explained, were directly opposite the London Palladium. During the interview, which was a great success, Vic informed the boys that his business partner, Eric Easton, was the manager of a band called The Rolling Stones, at which Four Steps Beyond took four steps back.

From the offices of the Eric Easton Organisation the band was instructed to travel down to Morden in Surrey to produce a demonstration disc. At the recording studios of RG Jones, the boys laid down two tracks, 'Keep Your Hands Off My Baby', and a self-penned song called 'The Artist'. The master tape was packaged and delivered to the agency in Little Argyle Street, where Vic Sutcliffe listened intently to both tracks, smiled, and immediately contracted Four Steps Beyond to the Easton Organisation.

Cock-a-hoop does not adequately describe the group's feelings. So much had been achieved in such a relatively short space of time. Within days of their return to Exeter, the band received an itinerary for a three-month tour of Denmark and Germany. Parents and girlfriends had to be told and received the news in differing ways. Mike's parents, Maureen and Jim, were rather subdued then took the wind from their excited seventeen-year-old son's sails by saying, 'You can't work abroad, you're too young.'

Mike's father was, of course, correct. However, a valid signed and witnessed passport application, along with a legal requirement that Mike, officially still a minor, report to the nearest British Embassy each week whilst on the Continent, would allow him to tour with the band. Much pleading and adolescent whingeing resulted in Jim's signature on the necessary documentation. A representative of the Easton Organisation countersigned the papers, and a British passport was issued in the name of Mr Michael Emery.

The imposing Carousel Club, in the Danish capital of Copenhagen, was the band's workplace for the initial four weeks of the tour. Mike faithfully complied with his conditions, and checked in with the Consulate on each of the first three weeks. A phone call from the London agency on the morning of their final gig at the Carousel, instructed the boys to, 'Pack your bags and make your way to the New York City Club in Vitten, near Dortmund in Germany, as soon as you finish at The Carousel tonight.' Luggage and personal effects were assembled, and last-minute souvenir hunting completed. Four Steps Beyond excelled at the club that evening, and their farewells to the staff, who by now were friends, were quite emotional. It was not until they were crossing the German border that Colin Drake said, 'Oi Mick, have you clocked in this week?'

Young Mick had forgotten to visit the British Embassy in their final week in Denmark. 'Bit late to do anything about it now,' murmured Alan Bryant, 'You'll have to sort it out in Germany.' Later that morning, the band arrived at Vitten and found the club without difficulty. Met by the owner, the boys were given directions to a house which they were to share with another British touring band for the next four weeks.

The band called the In Betweens represented the Jack Fallon Agency, whose offices were in the Wolverhampton area. Four Steps Beyond and their new mates hit it off immediately, with much light-hearted banter about dialects and such. The In Betweens were to play at the sister establishment to the New York Club, the Habanera, and were to be paid by monthly cheque, posted directly from Wolverhampton. Four Steps Beyond received their fees weekly, and in cash. Four Steps were constantly 'subbing' their Midlands colleagues, for which the In Betweens were obviously grateful. Several years later, Mike Emery was watching 'Top of the Pops' on TV, and was astounded to see the In Betweens performing their latest hit record under a new name – Slade.

The lads from the West Country played to full houses every night, and

The dressing room of the Carousel Club: (L–R) Geoff Cox, Alan Bryant, Roger Walker, Colin Drake, Mike Emery

received rave reviews. The one-month stint passed quickly, and the boys were sorry to leave. Their instructions for the final leg of the tour were, as they had been throughout, quite specific. Four Steps Beyond were to drive to a pre-booked guest-house approximately halfway between Vitten and the USAF base at Falda near Frankfurt. There they were to rest overnight before carrying on to Falda where they would entertain the airmen and airwomen during the next month.

The German couple, Herr and Frau Schmidt, who owned the little B&B, spoke a little English, and provided coffee and light refreshment for the tired but happy musicians. The events of the next ten minutes resembled a scene from a Hitchcock movie. The phone rang and when the landlady returned from answering it her face was ashen; lapsing into her native tongue she conveyed the contents of the phone call to her husband whose face took on a similar pallor.

'Not bad news I hope,' offered Roger Walker pleasantly. Protectively drawing his wife to his side, Herr Schmidt replied, 'That vas the police, for one of you they are looking, and here they will be coming soon.'

'Why should they want us?' said Geoff Cox, 'We haven't done anything.'
'When did you last report to a consulate Mike?' asked Alan Bryant.
'Oh Lord, said Mike, it must be five weeks ago now.'
'That's it then, said Alan, I think it's time we weren't here.'

Thanking the German couple profusely, the boys high-tailed it to the van and put as many kilometres as possible between themselves and the police.

Dopey and Pillock were two of the nicer forms of address used by the band when referring to a very sheepish Mike Emery during their hasty retreat from the guest-house. Mike 'surrendered' to the local constabulary at Dusseldorf where, in the presence of representatives from both German and British embassies, he was severely ticked off.

Four Steps Beyond were told that they would be allowed to remain in the country until they had fulfilled their existing contract, after which their work permits would be revoked. Further, the boys were informed that failure to leave Germany immediately on completion of their month's engagement at the airbase would result in certain, and much publicised deportation. Suitably chastened, Mike Emery dejectedly left the police station to the sound of his four colleagues hissing, 'Prat!'

Although the Americans were harder to please – there were jukeboxes in each mess filled with the latest releases from both sides of the Atlantic – Four Steps Beyond's intricate vocal harmonies won them over, and the final evening of their Continental adventure was one the boys would never forget. En route to the coast and the ferry their van began to overheat. The temperature gauge was rising at an alarming rate, the engine sounded terminally ill, and there appeared to be smoke emanating from the engine compartment. Pulling to the side of the autobahn, Roger Walker lifted the bonnet to see that some of the wiring was actually on fire. Showing great presence of mind, Roger calmly walked to the rear of the van, picked up three litre bottles of Coca Cola, shook the bottles vigorously, then removed the caps and put the fire out.

'Who's a clever boy then?' said Roger. He was talking to himself, the other four musicians being a hundred yards down the road. His father was contacted at his home in Exmouth, and sent sufficient funds to enable the lads to purchase another van locally, and thus continue their journey to the ferry port.

Back in the offices of the Easton Organisation, Vic Sutcliffe , the co-guarantor for Mike Emery's conduct while on the Continent, went predictably ballistic. Mike was informed that he could consider himself fortunate that public hangings no longer took place at Tyburn. The other four members of the group were also castigated and five very red-faced musicians left the building.

Although Four Steps Beyond continued to represent the Easton Organisation, appearing at the Talk of the Town and the Charlie Chester Club among other less notable venues, bookings from the agency gradually lessened. The boys decided to sever all links with Sutcliffe and Easton and returned to their Exeter roots.

Home once more, they tried to rebuild the fan-base they had once had. Lesley Ireland, the vocalist girlfriend of Colin Drake, occasionally guested with the group in an effort to vary the sound and style, but to no avail. The boys were disconcerted, and individually agreed that they needed a change. Four Steps Beyond broke up in 1967. Mike Emery changed not only band but also instrument, and joined Bill Greenhalgh's Orchestra as a bass guitarist.

On stage at St George's Hall, Exeter: (L–R) Geoff Cox, Alan Bryant, Roger Walker, Colin Drake, Mike Emery

Alan Bryant and Colin Drake became vocalist and bassist respectively with the Maurice Price Band. Geoff Cox's subsequent activities are unclear, but no doubt honourable.

Roger Walker joined his parents who had recently moved to the Merthyr Tydfil area in Wales, and it is not known whether he played the drums again.

Gary Kane and the Tornadoes

Without doubt, Gary Kane and the Tornadoes was the band that set the standard by which all other semi-professional outfits were judged.

Founded in 1957 by Michael and Norman, the sons of Frederick and Hilda Parr, the landlord and landlady of the John Bull (now The Artful Dodger) public house in the St David's area of Exeter, both boys had attended the Episcopal school in Dinham Road.

On completing his education, Norman, at the insistence of his father, started his working life with Exe Engineering at their works in Alphington Road. In the early part of 1944 he was drafted into the Manchester Regiment, serving with the machine gun battalion until late 1947. Michael was called up for National Service in 1955, and demobbed from the Devonshire Regiment two years later, spending much of the time in Germany. Prior to receiving his call-up papers, he had trained as a carpenter/joiner indentured to Wippell's, a company manufacturing ecclesiastical furniture at premises in Dinham Road. He returned there after demob.

Skiffle, the latest dance craze to arrive from America, was being played on the radio and in dance halls everywhere, and the fun-loving brothers – totally enamoured with the new breed of singers and musicians – decided to form a group.

The acquisition of a steel-strung, round-holed Spanish guitar and a simplistic book depicting chord shapes, together with several hours of diligent study,

The Tornadoes skiffle group at Totnes: (L–R) Mike Parr, Percy Turner, Ken Bassett, Harry Bovington, Norman Parr, Jenny Glanville

was to Michael proof positive that whilst he might never cause too many guitarists to awake from their slumbers screaming, he had become an adequate three-chord trickster.

The first person to 'benefit' from Mike's newly acquired skills was the gentleman who provided the in-house entertainment at the John Bull pub on Saturday evenings. The man, whose name sadly cannot be remembered, was at first quite happy with Mike's offer to strum along but problems arose from the outset. The pianist played 'sur noir' – on the black notes only – which put his stoic rendition of songs like 'Nellie Dean' and 'Down at the Old Bull and Bush' in flattened or sharpened keys.

Barely at the Grade 1 stage, Mike found great difficulty in matching his limited library of chords to anything the chap played. For his part, the ivory tinkler had never heard of the 'Rock Island Line' and was pretty indifferent to the fact that 'Chewing Gum loses its flavour when placed on a bed-post overnight'.

Brother Norman, reminiscent of Tom the cabin boy in the children's television programme 'Captain Pugwash', said nothing. The sash-cord on his tea-chest bass would produce any note required, providing of course that his hand was in the correct position. The unlikely trio did manage to play a few songs together eventually, and the as yet unidentified piano player was rather taken with Mike's voice. 'Clear as a bell, and he moves about a bit, he ought to do it for a living,' he thought.

These public performances served to strengthen the resolve of the brothers Parr and The Tornadoes skiffle group resulted. Ken Bassett, Ray Hill, and Harry Bovington, who worked with Mike at Wippell's, joined the group as drummer, rhythm guitarist, and washboard player respectively. Initially 'playing' biscuit tins and oil drums, Ken managed to assemble a cheap drum-kit within a few weeks. Young Ray Hill owned an inexpensive Spanish guitar and, although by no means a guitar ace, he could play more chords than Mike. Harry is thought to have borrowed the washboard from his mum.

When Percy Turner, a friend of Norman's girlfriend's brother *(sorry, that bit is a trifle confusing – author)* became the group's lead guitarist, the band were able to play practically any song that appointed vocalist Mike cared to sing. Tony 'Sax' Sayers occasionally augmented this fine body of men, but his stay with the group was short-lived.

Skiffle was not to everyone's taste, however. The John Bull regulars readily expressed their preference for a good old singsong and knees-up on a Saturday night, rather than the newfangled music that the teenagers were playing.

The Cowley Bridge Inn became the venue for The Tornadoes' practice sessions. The locals invariably witnessed these rehearsals, and the hat was often passed round in appreciation of their efforts. One girl, who was in the

They liked the Tornadoes in Totnes!

bar with some friends, complimented the boys on their performance and mentioned that she could play both the guitar and the banjo. Jenny Glanville was promptly invited to become a member of the group.

Thanks largely to frequent rehearsal and Mike's singing ability, the group began to receive requests to perform at other local pubs, village halls, church fêtes and the like. Norman fondly recalls an occasion when the group played during the interval at an Exeter Falcons speedway meeting, to an audience of nearly 3000 people.

He also remembers, although perhaps not quite as fondly, a time when The Tornadoes staged an impromptu show on the traffic island just outside the John Bull. The policeman who attended the incident on his bicycle gave the youngsters an earbashing and told them to clear off. Apparently the motorists loved the music but the tailback stretched almost to Cowley Bridge.

During the next few years there were many changes. Rock and roll was gradually phasing out skiffle, and Jenny Glanville had left the band to become Mrs Tony Lever. Norman Parr, having fetched, carried, cooked and bottle-

The Tornadoes at the Co-op Hall in Torquay

Mark Shannon and the Sunsets at Ford Hall in Newton Abbot.

washed at the Windsor Hotel owned by his parents and situated opposite St David's railway station, was now married and the proprietor of a small, but busy grocery shop in Union Street, in the St Thomas area of the city.

Percy Turner, an apprentice plumber with a penchant for all things electronic, had left the group to become the lead guitarist of The Corvettes, linking up with his old friend John Greenslade with whom he would later establish Exeter Sound Recordings. Ray Hill had also left the band; seeking a fresh challenge he had accepted an invitation from vocalist Tony Osborne, who was using the stage-name Mark Shannon, to join his new outfit The Sunsets with Robin Hatherley, Len Simpson, and Tommy Gibson. Ray would however, rejoin The Tornadoes in 1963.

Ken Bassett and Harry Bovington had simply come to the conclusion that they had better things to do. The musicians that supplanted virtually the entire original skiffle group were all accomplished players. Rock and roll had exploded on to the Exeter and East Devon music scene, and the new-look Tornadoes were ready for it.

Fronted by the immaculate Mike Parr, whose voice, had long since mellowed from soprano to tenor, the band featured Vic Palmer on lead guitar, rhythm guitarist Tony Smythe who was equally at home behind a drum-kit, and London-born drummer Tony Harper. From Exeter, bass guitarist Rod Squires, an assistant at a music shop in Bridge Street, joined the band briefly but was soon replaced by Alan Maggs.

Signed by Lionel Digby the owner of LMD Entertainments in 1959, The Tornadoes had arrived. At Lionel's insistence, all the members of the band adopted stage names. Mike Parr became Gary Kane and, at the time of writing, one cannot help but wonder who, other than his family and closest friends, would think to address him as Mike. He has graced the stage for more than forty years. He is Gary Kane and will always be so. Vic Palmer became Vic Diamond and Tony Smythe became Dean Hunter. Bass guitarist Alan Maggs chose the name Danny Ocean which was taken from a film

'Good old British Leyland':
(L–R) Alan Maggs, Tony
Harper, Vic Palmer, Tony
Smythe. On roof, Gary Kane

starring the legendary Frank Sinatra and in deference to his birthplace, drummer Tony Harper slipped easily into the guise of Tony London.

Voted the 'Best in the West' in both 1961 and 1962 by the hundreds of dance-goers at the Tuesday Rock Club, held at the Co-op hall in Torquay, The Tornadoes consolidated their position as one of the South West's most popular bands.

Gary and the band broke new ground when they became the first rock and roll outfit to play at the Great Hall in Devonshire House on the Exeter University campus, following which they made regular appearances to the site, both in their own right, and as the support band to many of the top British, and American touring acts.

When they were not playing 'second fiddle' to artists like rhythm and blues legend Bo Diddley, Acker Bilk and Shane Fenton, the boys were packing 'em in at the Grand Hotel in Dawlish, Exeter's Civic Hall, the Guildhall in Plymouth, and both the Town and Queen's halls in Barnstaple, to mention but a few.

Christmas entertainment at
the '400' ballroom

Occasionally, the South West had to survive without its favourite popsters. Tours of the United Kingdom were readily available to bands with the pedigree of The Tornadoes. Thus, when contracts were offered they were invariably accepted, and the lads enjoyed countless months 'on the road' with Billy Fury, Gerry and the Pacemakers, Eden Kane and many others. All was well with the world, and Gary Kane and the Tornadoes in particular – or was it?

Murphy's Law, stating that if something can go wrong, it will, applied itself toward the end of 1963. Vic Palmer, by this time an accomplished organist, had for some time wanted to lead his own band and left The Tornadoes to form The Rejects. Gary was disappointed of course but appreciated the motive behind Vic's departure, fully aware that musicians will always feel the need to explore pastures new. With that thought in mind, Gary picked up the telephone and rang Ray Hill to offer him the job of lead guitarist.

If Gary had been *disappointed* when Vic Palmer announced his decision to leave The Tornadoes, he was *mildly irritated* when Alan Maggs followed suit. The irritation turned to *abject annoyance* when he learned that the bass guitarist had teamed up with Vic in The Rejects. He felt let down. Within minutes however, he had philosophically resolved that The Tornadoes would continue to be a force on the local music scene no matter what! Formerly the bass guitarist with The Corvettes, Norman Vautier joined The Tornadoes within the week and remained with the band until the end of 1964 when he returned to Jersey following his marriage. His position in the group was filled by ex-Nightlight Dave Parsons who assumed the stage name Dave de Verrier. Experienced musicians, Ray Hill and Norman Vautier easily adapted to The Tornadoes' style, and the outfit continued much as before.

Two further changes took place in the winter of 1963. Drummer Tony London was having various private problems and left the band pro tem, and Dave Smale, whose previous outfit The Corvettes, had recently disbanded, was recruited in his stead. Dave's good friend and fellow Corvette John Greenslade was pleased to renew their on and off-stage amity, when he was invited to replace rhythm guitarist Tony Smythe who had 'walked out', following a difference of opinion with Ray Hill and Gary Kane.

Gary was the ultimate professional, demanding high standards of his band members. This may possibly have accounted for the many changes of personnel in those early years. Stage dress was compulsory, smoking and drinking during any performance forbidden. But Gary was fiercely loyal to his band. It is well documented that in 1965 he was offered a recording contract with a national recording company, but on learning that session musicians were to be used in preference to The Tornadoes, declined to take up the contract.

The Tornadoes with stand-in bass player Colin Smythe

The memorable – especially for football fans – year of 1966 saw a merger between Gary Kane and the Tornadoes and the Don Brooks' Combo. Formed specifically to meet the criteria specified by the management of the Grand Hotel in Torquay and for a duration of six months, the Don Kenton Orchestra comprised, trumpeter, trombonist, saxophonist and band leader Don Brooks alias Don Kenton, keyboard player Roy Edwards, saxophonist Les Pengelly, guitarist Ray Hill, bassist Dave de Verrier and prodigal drummer Tony London. With charisma to spare, front man and part-time bongos player Gary Kane demonstrated from the outset why Don Kenton (Brooks) had chosen to instigate the unlikely alliance.

Following the very successful summer season the unit disbanded. Don Brooks joined the Maurice Price Band, as did guitarist Ray Hill, with John Greenslade moving in the opposite direction by rejoining The Tornadoes.

Gary Kane, John Greenslade, whose aliases now included Johnny Scott and Johnny Solo, and Dave Parsons (de Verrier) were the backbone of an outfit that continued to delight audiences throughout the remainder of the 1960s and 70s.

An extended-play record sleeve from the late 1970s

Charity work featured regularly and heavily in The Tornadoes' calendar, from more formal functions like the Civic Ball at venues such as the Riviera Centre and the Imperial Hotel at Torquay, to the locally inspired events held to raise funds for individuals. Nor were their charitable activities confined to the county of Devon. A nine-month-old baby girl, who was suffering from, among other disorders, a heart condition, made a guest appearance at a gig in Somerset. Her parents had brought the little girl along to thank Gary and the boys for their assistance in funding the purchase of a machine to aid her respiratory system.

Whilst rock and roll remained The Tornadoes' great love, the band kept well abreast of chart entries. Additionally, the boys regularly performed numbers penned by the prolific song-writing team of lead guitarist John Greenslade and his wife June. There were songs like 'We are the Falcons', written for the Exeter Speedway Team, 'The Exeter City Football Song', with its nominal 'B' side written especially for Grecians footballing legend Fred Binney (a man whose love of soccer was matched only by his passion for rhythm and blues music) and a song dedicated to the city of Exeter entitled 'City of 1000 Dreams'. Recorded by Johnny Ramone, the record was distributed to towns and cities named Exeter, worldwide: there are at least four in North America in New Hampshire, California, Nebraska and Rhode Island, as well as Tasmania and Canada. There can be few bands in the Exeter and East Devon area that have not at some juncture recorded a song written by June and John.

The early 1980s brought about a mini-revival of music from the swinging 60s; true, the songs had been digitally remastered (recording studio jargon meaning that synthesisers have been added, the tempo has been 'upped', and the tune now bears only a passing resemblance to the classic original) but

In an English country garden: (L–R) John West, Gary Kane, Ian Burgess, Dave Parsons, John Greenslade

The Tornadoes were once more performing chart-topping material, relieved of the burden of rehearsal.

The ever-youthful Gary Kane continued to entertain audiences until New Year's Eve 1997, surrounding himself with well-travelled and competent musicians like John West, Rod Allcock, Derek Shrubb, Ray Pope, Ray Hill, Bud Street, Ian Burgess, Steve Glover (who once nearly missed a gig at Burgh Island when the tide came in) and numerous others. Gary modestly maintains that his success was wholly due to the musicians standing alongside him, together with two previously unmentioned lads, Trevor Cross and Vince Orchard. Roadies with The Tornadoes at differing times, Trevor and Vince were both a huge asset to the band.

Four decades after his humble start at the John Bull pub, Gary took the decision to retire from the music scene, thinking perhaps that it might be nice to spend a Christmas with the family, or maybe aboard the other love of his life, his boat, *Tornado*.

However, the 'Kane' name lives on in the field of entertainment throughout Devon. Gary's son Kevin is well known for his appearances as a DJ in local clubs and as a presenter on the county's premier commercial radio station. You might even say he really is 'a chip off the old block'.

The Graded Grains formerly The Spartans

It was a popular television advertisement for a well-known flour, featuring a little chap called Fred dressed completely in black with matching bowler hat, that brought the catchphrase 'Graded grains make finer flour' into millions of households. Formerly from Exeter, now living in Crediton, guitarist, John Gregory maintains that 'Finer Flowerpot Flyers make Graded Grains'.

The 'Flowerpot Flyers' were a group of cycle speedway enthusiasts, formed with one exception by pupils of Hele's School in Quarry Lane, Exeter, the 'odd man out' being Christopher Forte who attended Winslade School. The boys created their track, practised and raced against other teams, at the Flower Pot playing fields in the St Thomas area, from whence they took their name.

On Saturday nights the boys were generally to be found at the St Matthew's Youth Club in Newtown, Exeter, standing on chairs, playing 'air guitar', and miming to the songs that were in the Hit Parade by The Beatles, Gerry and the Pacemakers, and many more.

In 1963, aged just fifteen, five members of the 'Flyers' decided that, rather than mime to the discs being played on the youth club's Dansette record player, and being far too old to ride bicycles, they would form their own pop group. By kind permission of Chris Forte's family, a meeting was held at their ice-cream factory in Preston Street, Exeter, where it was agreed that John Gregory would play lead guitar, Brian Sandy would be rhythm guitarist, and Roger Collett the lead vocalist. Chris Forte was nominated as bass guitarist, leaving Tommy Searle to play the drums.

The selection of a name for the band was a drawn-out affair. Fifty per cent

It's his fault it's broken …

of the suggestions could neither be spelt nor put into print, and from the other half only two were thought to be suitable. From this short-list of two names, The Cossacks, and The Spartans (the title of a tune recorded by Sounds Incorporated), the latter was chosen. By various means, each member got together the money needed for an instrument. John Gregory set the pace by selling his Meccano set and racing bike to finance his first guitar.

The Spartans' first public performance, some twelve months later, was to an enthusiastic audience of young people in the church hall, which hosted the Mount Pleasant Youth Club. John recalls that providing the song fell within the four chords or less category the boys would certainly attempt to play it. All self-taught musicians, The Spartans had made the transition from a hobby band to a semi-professional working outfit, by regular rehearsal and a fierce determination to succeed.

Eighteen-year-old Humphrey Loram, who lived in the Alphington area of the city, was a good friend, and a keen supporter of The Spartans. Ever-present at their gigs, Humphrey volunteered to act as the band's roadie if and when the boys 'got mobile'. Chris Forte, using plenty of nepotistic charm, obtained permission for the band to use a van, owned by the Forte's company, to transport themselves and their equipment to and from engagements. The vehicle, a 15cwt (approximately 0.75tk) Commer was, all things considered, fairly reliable. There were occasions, however, such as when the Commer was being serviced or repaired, when The Spartans would arrive at the venue in a glass-sided van festooned with plywood ice-cream cones, to the tune of 'Greensleeves' and with driver Humphrey grinning broadly. Humphrey's grin became virtually perpetual when, in late 1964, John Gregory persuaded him to buy, and learn to play, an electric organ.

A willing pupil, Humphrey became a member of The Spartans in mid-1965, replacing rhythm guitarist Brian Sandy, and made his debut on 4 June at the Royal Hotel in Dawlish.

Well, it made Abbey Road famous didn't it?

During the next two years there were several changes in the band's line-up. John, Chris, Roger and Tommy had completed their secondary education and were now, like Humphrey in full-time employment or at a college of further education. Their circle of friends widened, and the four lads began to drift apart. Janet Perks was added to the group for a short time as vocalist, and organist Graham Sclater was drafted in to replace Humphrey Loram, but both the interest and enthusiasm was gone, and The Spartans just 'faded away'.

We're off to Butlins! (L–R) Cliff Andrews, John Gregory and Bud Street

The close and long-standing friendship that existed between John Gregory and Ian 'Bud' Street had begun at school and continued into their college days. Bud, already exhibiting signs of becoming one of those most dangerous of breeds, a clever *and* competent bass player, and John, had long toyed with the idea of forming a band that was good enough to earn its living from music. Deciding that the new band should initially be a trio, word was spread that a new group, as yet unnamed and seeking to turn professional, needed a drummer. From more than 20 auditions and rehearsals with numerous drummers, local boy Cliff Andrews was selected.

John Gregory had already chosen a name for the new group, but prohibited its use until he received an answer from the entertainments manager at Butlins Holiday Camp in Minehead, Somerset, with whom he was negotiating a two-, or possibly three-week contract, to kick-start their career. In the meantime, the trio would come smartly to attention and answer their names if someone shouted, 'Clockwork Orange'.

On 29 July 1967, the lads took the stage at Butlins, Minehead as professional musicians for the first time, using the name about which the band had previously been so secretive, The Graded Grains. Paid £20 each per week, they were issued with identity cards which, in addition to the more obvious reasons of security, allowed them to buy food and drink at subsidised prices while on site. Accommodation was not included in the boys' salary, and they were resigned to sleeping in the van, which was parked outside the camp perimeter.

In October of that year – just as The Mustangs and Four Steps Beyond had done some years previously – The Graded Grains embarked on a six-month tour of Germany. In essence, the tour was to entertain the American Army troops at their many bases throughout Germany, and the contract stipulated that the band would feature a female vocalist. Local girl Lesley Ireland, who had guested with several bands in the Exeter area, agreed to accompany the Grains for the duration of the tour only.

Lesley's, and the boys' first overseas gig was at the enlisted men's club, on the US Army base in Ludwigsburg, near Stuttgart. The reception was favourable, and set the scene for the remainder of the tour. The Grains, albeit with a changed line-up, were to return to Europe in the near future, on a tour that took in not only Germany, but also France and Italy.

The Graded Grains, 1969 vintage

Following the tour Cliff Andrews became concerned that the work schedule had lessened somewhat, and decided to leave. A telephone call to old friend and founding member of The Spartans, Tommy Searle, quickly solved the problem of a replacement. Organist Terry Pascoe followed Tommy into the Grains, completing what was arguably the best of any previous, or future line-up musically.

Cliff's departure was possibly a little premature. The Grains became renowned for the quality and exuberance of their performances, and the diary rapidly filled. From 1968 to 1970, The Grains spent almost as much time on the Continent as they did in the UK, often working with or near another band from Exeter, The Magic Children. Both the vocalist and the drummer of the 'Children' were well known to the Grains. Roger Collett, like John Gregory and Tommy Searle, had been a founding member of The Spartans, and drummer John Carpenter a good friend of many years' standing. During this period also, the Grains had the pleasure of working with 'supergroups' Cream and Traffic, in addition to many other top-rated acts like Free and The Move.

The German tour of 1970 was to be the last for Bud Street and John Gregory. Boredom tinged with a little homesickness, prompted their decision to shed the mantle of professional entertainer, in favour of semi-professional status. Roger Collett and John Carpenter who returned to Exeter with John and Bud felt the same. Tommy Searle and organist Terry Pascoe joined lead guitarist Dave Meakal and bass player Paul 'Harry' Crane in The Magic Children and continued as professional musicians.

Some twelve months later Bud Street was asked to become bass player with Gary Kane's Tornadoes, without doubt the most popular band in the area at this time. The lucrative offer was one that Bud, now with the added responsibilities of a wife and child, could not refuse, said as much in discussion with John Gregory, John C, and Roger Collett, and so The Graded Grains collectively called it a day.

Contraband, the brainchild of John Gregory and the result of twelve months of experimentation and rehearsal, was launched on to the Mid and East Devon music scene in 1972. Keeping to The Graded Grains format, John had cabaret very much on his mind. The other members were organist Trevor Pugsley, bass guitarist Tony Curtis and John Carr on drums.

The band quickly became established on the local circuit, and it was not until the middle of 1973 that there were changes in personnel. Trevor and John Carr were replaced by rhythm guitarist Trevor Inch and much-travelled drummer Gary Gray, and 'the smoke went up the chimney just the same'. John Gregory loved music generally, and thoroughly enjoyed his time with Contraband. Nevertheless, the outfit never quite evoked the same emotions that he had experienced with The Graded Grains. John was delighted, therefore, when he was asked to guest with The Tornadoes, and leapt at the chance to reunite with his old friend Bud Street. John slotted in perfectly and, but for the unwavering loyalty shown to lead guitarist John Greenslade by Gary Kane, would have joined The Tornadoes on a permanent basis.

When, for reasons unspecified, Bud Street and drummer Dave Smale left The Tornadoes, Bud rang John Gregory who immediately terminated his membership of Contraband and suddenly The Graded Grains were back. Dave Smale moved on after a nine-month stint with the 'Grains Mk II', and several drummers, including Rob Shaw and Steve Orgée, ran the 'engine room' before finally in 1976, Gary Gray left Contraband to team up once more with John Gregory.

The period in which Steve Orgée featured is certainly worth a mention. The Graded Grains featured on BBC radio programme 'Morning Sou'West', TV's Spotlight, and on local radio 'live from the Devon County Show'. Well-rehearsed comedy routines were gradually added to the already impressive stage presentation, and comparisons were often made to the highly talented and amusing Grumbleweeds.

The Graded Grains

In this mode, the boys continued to entertain audiences in the South West throughout the remainder of the 1970s and well into the 80s. Although John Gregory insists that the Grains were not perhaps the best musically, with a top-quality sound system, state-of-the-art lighting, a basketful of props and roadies like Rod, Paul, Clive, Mike, Malcolm and others – working just as hard, sometimes harder than the band – the Graded Grains fully deserved the accolade of the region's top cabaret/comedy group.

'The time has come,' John Gregory said, 'to think of many notions,
Like snooker tables, balls and cues, and alcoholic potions.'

To allow John Gregory and Bud Street – who had become business partners in the acquisition of Crediton Snooker Club (now Potters) – time to get the enterprise ready for the official opening, The Graded Grains were disbanded in the friendliest of fashions after a show on 31 January 1986.

The Harlequins

The song 'Gypsies, Tramps and Thieves' released in the early 1970s by American songstress Cher, opens with the words 'I was born in the wagon of a travelling show.'

The words might have been penned for Gareth Whitehead, although his mother Hilda certainly never danced for monetary reward, and his father Dietlof John – known to all as Garry – whilst occasionally enjoying a tipple did not peddle a dubious cure-all called Doctor Goode.

Mr and Mrs Whitehead were showmen and Garry was born and raised in a travelling fair. He recalls that he had no formal education but was blessed with the experience of life itself, being literally born into the entertainment business.

At eleven years old he bought his first guitar – a round-holed Spanish affair with steel strings – and attempted to play along with the records that were broadcast nightly through the fairground's massive PA system. The resulting noise and some ill-advised backchat turned the normally placid Hilda into a decidedly edgy lady, and the lightweight instrument was reduced to matchwood when she hit her misbehaving offspring over the head with it.

Mum, of course, was almost as upset as Garry as with the exception of this isolated incident she was extremely proud and supportive of her son. But it was more than two years before Garry acquired his next guitar, a Lux acoustic costing 14 guineas (£14.70).

In 1960 he joined his grandfather's jute recycling business, having decided to make Exeter his permanent home. He greatly missed the travelling but took comfort from the thought of forming, or joining, an established band, and very sensibly practised daily, playing along with records by Cliff Richard, The Shadows, Elvis Presley and later The Beatles. With the help of sheet music, which normally included the chord structure, and regular visits to local dance halls to watch his two favourite groups The Tornadoes and The Corvettes, for whose lead guitarist Percy Turner he had the utmost respect, Garry became an extremely proficient guitarist.

His first electric guitar, a Burns Sonic, complete with a Truvox amplifier that was a present from his mum and dad, costing a staggering £75, spurred him into action and brought almost immediate results. On the Sunday morning after acquiring his new equipment Garry and his mate Tony Osborne – later to become one of Exeter's best-known vocalists – won the weekly talent competition held at the '400' Club in Torquay with their rendition of two

© 1963 By D. J. Whitehead

Front cover of a Harlequins 'Jiving licence'

popular songs, 'Only Sixteen' and the Tennessee Ernie Ford classic 'A Hundred Pounds of Clay'.

After winning the competition for four weeks consecutively, Garry and Tony were asked to refrain from taking part to give other acts a chance.

The talent competition prompted Garry to form his own group, which he decided should be called The Harlequins. He recalls that the band's first gig was in 1963 and was held at the Village Hall in Alphington, Exeter; also that he booked the venue, and both advertised and ran the function himself. Unfortunately, he cannot remember the original line-up. So here follows an attempt to mention every guitarist, vocalist, and drummer that took the stage as a member of The Harlequins, with apologies if the text is chronologically flawed.

It is known that The Harlequins soon after formation comprised band leader and lead guitarist Garry Whitehead, rhythm guitarist Andy Barnes, who would later be replaced by Mike Emery, bassist Colin Drake, drummer Tommy Gibson and vocalist Alan 'Kaiser' Bryant. Dietlof John (Garry Snr) was a tower of strength to the young musicians. Acting as both manager and driver, he also provided the band with its first PA system. The top-quality equipment, manufactured by a company called Vortexion, had previously been used on the fairground and this, together with a microphone that had also been donated by the benevolent gentleman, was used for vocals.

Regular rehearsals – which were normally held in the foyer of the Savoy cinema by kind permission of manager Bob Parker – along with some competent live performances, articles in the press and word of mouth, ensured that The Harlequins steadily gained in popularity. In addition to the self-run functions at the Civic, and St George's Hall, the boys performed at

On stage at Bodmin Town Hall

the Athena Club, the University of Exeter, and many town and village halls in the Exeter and East Devon area. Entertainment agents Trevor and Billie George, John White and Lionel Digby ensured that the group was kept busy. They also crossed the border into both Somerset and Cornwall, with Bodmin Town Hall, Tabbs, and the Bamboo clubs in Redruth being three of the band's favourite venues.

One excursion to Cornwall proved costly. After an enjoyable gig at Tabbs in Redruth, lead guitarist Garry, driving his grandfather Jimmy Rowe's elderly Bedford J2 van, pulled into a garage near Okehampton to buy a carton of milk. Unfortunately, the automatic machine had been vandalised, leaving the Harlequins thirsty as well as tired. Garry got back into the van and headed for home. Whether his reactions were numbed by fatigue or whether he fell asleep at the wheel is unclear, but the van rolled over and amidst a shower of sparks slid along the road, coming to rest inches from an oncoming car. The three occupants of the car assisted the battered and bruised but otherwise unhurt Harlequins to right the van, and the last leg of the journey was completed by a somewhat more verbose set of musicians. A survey of the damage the next morning revealed that not only was the van's bodywork a sorry sight, but three amplifiers had been damaged beyond repair.

Following Tommy Gibson's exodus, both Tony Harper and Geoff Perkins drummed with the group prior to Roger Walker taking the 'hot seat', a position he still held when Alan Bryant and Mike Emery left the band to form the Secrets Mk II.

Bill Grant, formerly the bass player with The Buccaneers joined The Harlequins – the outfit with a bigger turnover of staff than Sainsbury's – replacing Mike Emery, and immediately suggested that his mate Tom Willmott become the 'Quins' front man. A likeable character, Tom had been singing from an early age following a visit to the fairground on Haven Banks,

Back right, Tom Willmott;
front right, Garry Whitehead

The Western College Players present 'It's a Record'

Exeter, with a school friend, 'Paddy' Flavin. Paddy had listened to Tom singing along to the records being played over the fairground's Tannoy system, and suggested that he join a rock group. Tom subsequently became a member of The Buccaneers and met bass player Bill.

But true to form and in keeping with the band's apparent 'rolling staff' policy, Bill left the group shortly after Tom's recruitment, with Dave Mulvihill taking up the challenge. Dave and Andy Barnes would later leave The Harlequins to form the very noteworthy Bluesounds.

Lead guitarist Garry enjoyed composing music and together with his brother-in-law Tommy Gardner, also a former travelling showman and an excellent lyricist, wrote many surprisingly good songs. The duo was successful from the outset. The first offering from the pen of Exeter's answer to Rogers and Hammerstein a song called 'It's Just a Matter of Time' took first place at a competition held at The Den in Teignmouth. The follow-up, a tune entitled 'It's Wonderful', was used together with several other original compositions, in a play performed by the Western College Players, a drama group from Plymouth, called 'It's a Record'. The programme notes credited Garry, Tommy, and The Harlequins with the music, and also gave a special mention to the lady in charge of props – a Miss Angela Rippon.

The first major song-writing triumph came when 'There Must Be Something Wonderful About Fighting' won a national competition organised by the BBC. Robin Hall and Jimmy McGregor performed the song on a BBC North television programme, and subsequently recorded it on the Fontana record label. Interestingly, The Harlequins recorded the original demo in the foyer of the Savoy cinema.

A good friend to the Harlequins and applauded by them for his time and patience, John Shepherd from Whimple was the man responsible for recording the majority of the band's demo tapes, while Jeremy Fry from Bath financially backed the band's first professional recording.

Swedish singing star Kurt Borkman achieved notability with a Whitehead/Gardner original called 'I'd give the World'. Ron Richards, the man behind most of the Hollies hits, produced the song at Abbey Road Studios in London with a 40-piece orchestra.

Can't beat a bit of publicity!

Garry and Tommy received national acclaim when the late Malcolm Roberts reached number three in the British Hit Parade (charts) with one of their songs which was recorded on the now defunct Major Minor label, and as if to demonstrate the song-writing partnership's flexibility, 'The Chewton Mendip Love-In' was recorded live in Bristol by Adge Cutler and The Wurzels.

With the possible exception of husband-and-wife team John and June Greenslade, there were few composers locally who could match Garry and Tommy's prolific output. As if reliving their childhood days, Tommy and Garry, together with the other Harlequins, found themselves back on the road, regularly performing to audiences in the South, the South East, and the Midlands.

Notwithstanding his love of song-writing, Garry continued to enjoy the 'bread and butter gigs' locally. So far, 1963 had been a memorable year. The year drew to its close somewhat sadly, however, when on the evening of 22 November at a dance in Tiverton at which The Harlequins were performing, the gig was interrupted by a policeman, who gravely announced to all present that the President of the United States of America, John F Kennedy had been assassinated.

The fascination with song-writing and musical arrangements eventually took second place to an exciting ecological project, pioneered, researched and developed by the composing couple from an original Tommy Gardner idea. The concept involved the shredding of paper for use as animal bedding. The universally accepted and therapeutic nature of the product resulted in a new factory in Exeter and, following a visit to the premises by HRH Prince Philip, a royal warrant was granted to the company.

The business took precedence over The Harlequins and the group quietly disbanded. In the four years during which The Harlequins became so popular, all of the following played an important role: guitarists John Ffoulkes, Dave Sercombe, Alan Maggs, Derek Luscombe, Ray Hill, John Greenslade, John Bridges and Len Simpson; university students and guitarists Ian Gillette and Brian Ellery; also students, keyboard player John Arnold, Eric the drummer and saxophonist Jason, drummer Roger Kelly, and vocalists John Orton and Mike Guard.

As mentioned at the top of this biography, the author has made a concerted effort to include all former members of The Harlequins and hopes that the foregoing is a valiant effort, with apologies to any that have been missed.

Founder member, band leader, and lead guitarist Garry left the UK, initially on a business trip, discovered that the climate in Palm Beach, Florida, was just what the doctor ordered and settled there. Tom Willmott joined a band called The Deetones – an eight-piece dance band who were to enjoy a residency at the Caprice Club in Exeter when The Maurice Price Band moved to Tiffany's.

The Deetones comprised organist Derek Ledbrook, saxophonists Derek Lock and Derek Hutchings – the name Derek obviously contributing to the band's name – trombonist Peter Rowe, guitarist Tony Hornsby, a bass player who was known only as Gino, vocalist Tom Willmott and a man who was to become one of Tom's greatest friends both on and off stage, drummer Ken Butler.

Ken, sadly no longer with us, is fondly remembered for the following incidents. Having arrived early with other members of The Deetones for a function at Tiffany's, Ken set his drum-kit up as usual, noticed it was no longer raining and with some of the boys decided to take the air. Standing nonchalantly outside the entrance, the drummer filled his favourite briar and genially nodded to the doorman who was about to fold up the awning above the door.

As it returned to the closed position, gallons of water cascaded down, drenching the hapless drummer. Ken had to be physically restrained from assaulting the doorman, not for the drenching he had received, but because he had only just got his pipe going.

Ken worked as a sales representative and was allowed to use his company car 'out of hours'. Returning from a gig in North Devon, with the boot and back seats filled with his drum-kit and accessories, Ken and Tom Willmott were within sight of Eggesford Station, rounding a long left-hand bend, when they saw a young lad waving frantically from his position on top of the hedge. Winding his window down, Ken drove past the boy shouting, 'Sorry mate – we're full up!' Round the corner he collided with the teenager's broken-down Mini. The insurance company wrote off both the company car and the Mini, and Ken lost his job, but as he later stoically remarked, 'At least the kit was OK.'

Top: (L–R) Ken Butler, Tom Willmott, Derek Ledbrook, Gino; Below: (L–R) Derek Lock, P Rowe, Derek Hutchings, Tony Hornsby

The Hip Hooray Good Times Band
Latterly known as The Hip Hooray Band

The break-up of The Bluesounds was an amicable but protracted affair. Lead guitarist Andy Barnes, having started his own hairdressing business, had left the band in August 1968, and rhythm guitarist John Bridges was helping out any outfit that required his services. Tony Fowler had stored his fast-oxidising drum-kit in a vacant corner of the garage and was looking forward to a well-earned holiday.

L–R: J Bridges, Dave Mulvihill, Tony Fowler, Andy Barnes

Bass player and band leader Dave Mulvihill wanted to form another group and had placed an advertisement in the window of Bill Greenhalgh's shop (the musician's answer to the Labour Exchange/Job Centre). Notwithstanding his entrepreneurial and bass-playing skills, Dave would always be remembered for sacking drummer Steve Upton who, following his departure from The Bluesounds, co-founded a group called The Empty Vessels, from which evolved… Wishbone Ash.

Dave had played rock and roll with The Harlequins, and rhythm and blues with The Bluesounds. The new band, Dave decided, should encompass the whole spectrum of popular music including soul, for which he needed a brass section.

In September 1968, The Bluesounds comprised lead guitarist Robin Phillips, an easygoing guy with an amazing talent for musical arrangement, drummer Roger Pike, Dave Mulvihill, saxophonist Mike Watts and, for a few months, trumpet player Steve Baker.

Three months later, sixteen-year-old Bob Darlison, keyboard player and the brother of experienced bassist Richard 'Dick' Darlison, completed phase one of the Mulvihill master plan. A friend of Robin Phillips, Ray Beavis, took Steve's front-line position in January 1969; Ray and Robin had previously worked together in a band named The In-Sect.

The Hip Hoorays in the early days

Dance promoters and agents were contacted, and advised that The Bluesounds now featured brass and keyboard. One such agent, Mike Deakin – a well-known and highly respected North Devonian with whom The Bluesounds had enjoyed a long-standing working relationship – was mightily impressed with both the sound and the presentation of numbers done by outfits like Blood Sweat and Tears, Chicago, and The Moody Blues, but probably less enamoured with the increase in price.

Mike and Dave Mulvihill debated this potential stumbling block at length before a mutual understanding was reached i.e. Dave won. Mike Deakin

The boys at Pontin's, Brixham

was, however, responsible for renaming the band. Quite how he came up with The Hip Hooray Good Times Band no one knows but presumably he was influenced by outfits like Geno Washington and the Ram Jam Band, who were riding high at the time. He appeared to have little difficulty in 'selling' the band, and became their sole representative in North Devon, Somerset and Dorset, a mutually acceptable alliance that lasted for many years.

In November 1972, the boys attended an audition at the Labour Club, Clifton Hill, Exeter. Staged by the Mecca group, these were to select entertainment for the 1973 summer season at Pontin's Dolphin Holiday Camp in Brixham. Once in their stage wear, the six-piece went into a tremendous routine which had fingers snapping, feet tapping and smiles on influential faces.

They were duly informed that they could consider themselves conditionally booked for the forthcoming season, and that a contract would be issued, providing that the manager at the Brixham camp was also in favour. In February of the following year, Hip Hooray visited the camp, once again donned stage dress and performed a similar set for the manager, Derek Hardy. They were 'home and dry'. In conversation with Dave Mulvihill later that evening, Derek said that he had been impressed not only with the musical content but also, because the band had 'dressed for the performance'. The Hip Hooray Good Times Band were to appear at Pontin's holiday camps for the next 15 summer seasons, consecutively.

Although the band consisted of proficient and cohesive musicians, the overall sound was largely attributable to Derek Tolman. An electronics boffin, he serviced and repaired amplifiers, echo-units, microphones and the like at Bill Greenhalgh's, was a friend of the band and frequently travelled to gigs with them.

In Derek's company, and whilst playing at the Fiesta Club in Plymouth, the boys were becoming more frustrated by the minute. The dance floor, filled to capacity when the DJ was spinning discs, would empty after the band had played two or three songs. Normally one of the most popular bands to be booked there, they could not comprehend the reason for the 'space to let' sign invisibly appearing in the centre of the room. Derek Tolman thought he had the answer. 'It's the sound in the subconscious,' he said to Robin Phillips during the interval. 'We'll try "miking-up" the bass drum and high-hat.' Derek duly placed microphones in the appropriate positions around the drum-kit, the band took the stage for their next set, and watched agog as the audience teemed on to the dance floor.

Derek became the band's sound engineer from that moment onward. In the following weeks he built a mixing console with sufficient capacity to accept all the microphones, and allow total amplification of the drums.

Human nature being what it is, it is unimaginable that a band, be it professional or semi-professional, will not at some time experience personnel changes. This is obviously magnified when the outfit in question is a sextet and The Hip Hooray Good Times Band membership altered many times during their exceptionally long run.

Ray Beavis, initially a trumpet player with the band before discovering that his real love was the saxophone, had moved out of the area and become a professional musician of some standing. Organist Bob Lynch had replaced Bob Darlison and would remain as the 'keys man' until August 1975. The brass section was continually astir. Saxophonists Jim Ridler, Grenville Downing, Marius Rudnic and Scottish migrant 'Mac' Rae all played an important part in the band's development during its formative years.

The eagerly awaited summer season at the holiday camp in Brixham fully lived-up to the boys' expectations. Fun-packed and with rarely a dull moment, the band constantly encountered fresh challenges. One such was 'Can you play a Royal Empress Tango?' It wasn't a question but an order! Three bus-loads of enthusiastic ballroom dancers from Wales were naturally bent on enjoying their holiday and they were determined that The Hip Hooray Good Times Band was going to live up to its name. To their credit, the boys got an amiable couple to hum the tune then played it. The tempo, however, was decidedly suspect.

One couple gliding silkily past the front of the stage said, 'There's fast isn't it?', while another pair insisted that the band were playing too slowly. 'We'll sort it out by tomorrow evening,' said Dave Mulvihill, who privately thought that the Earth Wind and Fire version they had just played was perfectly acceptable. Peter Tolman, brother of sound engineer Derek and an excellent ballroom dancer, was contacted the next day. Peter produced a list of the accepted speeds for the majority of popular ballroom dances, in which was included the Royal Empress Tango at 32 beats per minute. When the boys performed the number that same evening, Anglo-Welsh harmony was

Oh what a night!

immediately restored, although Dave still liked their original version At the end of the season, which the boys declared had been an unqualified hoot it was back to the 'bread-and-butter gigs'.

At the end of the summer season of 1974, guitarist Robin Phillips announced his intention to leave the bank where he worked, to become a professional musician.

Dave Mulvihill had secured a contract with the Mecca group to perform seven nights per week, at a function room called The Chimes behind the Ring of Bells public house in Northampton, and commuting from Exeter on a daily basis, whilst not impossible would have been uneconomical and tiring. With the exception of band leader Dave, who elected to travel to Northampton every day for a week or so before finally leaving Wheatons, the rest of the band emulated their lead guitarist and turned professional immediately.

The Hip Hooray Good Times Band dispensed with the words Good Times when it was found that it would not fit on to a poster to advertise their forthcoming appearance at the Steering Wheel Club in Dorchester. This truncation of identity coincided with Dave Mulvihill's first meeting with Don Jones. A virtuoso alto-saxophone player and formerly a member of the world-famous Ambrose Orchestra, Don had for some time worked for the Mecca group, but was seeking to set up his own Entertainments Agency. Dave, in London at the offices of Mecca to discuss further contracts, was introduced to Don and the pair subsequently became firm friends.

In 1975 and 1976, the boys had only to concern themselves with the period between October and the following April, Pontin's being their home for the twenty-odd weeks during the summer season. In 1977, a seemingly innocuous telephone call changed that routine and catapulted them into mainstream entertainment and the bright lights.

Don Jones had been badly let down by a band. Badly is probably the wrong word because the outfit had made an excellent job of dropping him in it. An apologetic spokesman had informed Don that due to unforeseen circumstances, they could not honour a contract to appear at a venue in Swindon the following evening. After a few choice swear words and a look at his desk diary he noted that all his regular bands were booked up but spotted the words Hip Hooray Band, Exeter.

In a last-gasp attempt to get a good band, Don explained his predicament to Dave Mulvihill. Although presently enjoying a couple of well-earned rest days and 'completely underwhelmed' with the fee of eighty pounds (which included travelling costs), Dave agreed to assist his friend and confirmed that the Wiltshire gig would be covered. Don was to repay the favour in spades.

The Empire Ballroom in Leicester Square, London

Shortly after the Swindon booking Don again contacted his friend with his thanks and an invitation to bring the band to London to attend an audition. He would not reveal who it would be for but did let on that it would be a prestigious venue.

The audition was to be held in an Italian restaurant in the heart of London, and the boys were a little surprised to find on their arrival that they appeared to be the only band present. It transpired that Don Jones had recommended the Hip Hooray Band to Peter Smith the Managing Director of Thorn-EMI Leisure, and he had asked for the audition. From the restaurant the band were escorted to the 3000-capacity Empire ballroom in Leicester Square, to be informed that they were to take second billing to the renowned Ray McVay Big Band in co-residency for one month, with the option of a further four weeks' work if everything worked out as anticipated. Awe-struck, they could only nod their assent as they watched the large circular stage silently revolve through 180 degrees, taking Ray McVay's gear backstage. The Hip Hooray's equipment was quickly set up up on the vacant half of the stage, and the boys launched into a fairly unnecessary demonstration number, Peter Smith having already made his decision to employ the lads from Devon.

Now that's a big band!

The mechanical dais enabled the McVay and Hip Hooray bands to perform the slickest of changeovers. Counted in by Ray McVay, the two outfits would start playing his band's closing number simultaneously. Then the revolving stage was activated, bringing the Hip Hooray band into view and taking the McVay Big Band backstage, the slight decrease in volume being the only difference.

In December 1977, the boys were contracted to play at the Romeo & Juliet Club in Bristol. The contract for the five-month gig which would take the band neatly into April 78 and their usual summer season at Pontin's, was issued by Thorn-EMI who had decided not to renew the R&J Club lease to the Mecca group. So popular was the Hip Hooray Band at the Bristol venue, that Thorn-EMI booked the outfit for their Romeo & Juliet clubs in both Derby and Hull during the next two years. Band leader Dave Mulvihill's office work had been reduced considerably. He now needed to make two entries only in his diary – Pontin's, and Romeo & Juliet's to span the entire year.

On completion of the summer season in 1979 the Hip Hooray Band was told to 'Go to Hell'. Far from being derogatory, Hell was a town in Norway and the opening gig of a thirteen-week tour, during which the band would back Sally Sagoe who until recently had been in the cast of *Jesus Christ Superstar* in London's West End. Dave recalls that the Norwegians were generally fun-loving, quiet and peaceful, and that when the tambourine and maracas were 'stolen' from the corner of the stage, they were later found undamaged in a plastic carrier bag tied to the rear door handles of the van.

Six double-oh sevens

The boys enjoyed their stint and were even more pleased when, at the conclusion of the tour, they were instructed to drive to Copenhagen to play at two clubs, the Jomfruburett and the Virgin's Cave. Events at both venues are noteworthy. On the evening of their gig at the Jomfruburett, the Danish Olympic rowing team was celebrating their placing in a recently held inter-national competition, and treated each of the musicians to a bottle of Chivas Regal.

At the Virgin's Cave the lads were contracted to perform from 10pm until 6am, playing for thirty minutes, then resting for the same time, throughout the eight-hour stint. All bands appearing at the Cave were challenged to play without a break for the whole shift, with a gratis slap-up meal as a reward. At that time no outfit had ever claimed their free meal. Neither did the Hip Hooray Band!

When asked to specify the single most memorable event in his musical career, Dave Mulvihill stated simply 'New Year's Eve 1980, Dubai'. The booking from old friend Don Jones involved an 8000-mile round trip from Exeter to the United Arab Emirates via Heathrow, to play at a party to be held at the newly opened Dubai International Hotel owned by the Sheik of Dubai. The sheik required that the band play from 10pm on New Year's Eve until 3am on New Year's Day, and stipulated that 'Auld Lang Syne' be played.

The six-piece Hip Hooray Band, guitarists Dave Mulvihill and Robin Phillips, pianist Brian 'Fingers' Kirby, drummer Roger Pike, trumpet player Grenville Downing, saxophonist John Snell together with two female singers, Sally Sagoe who had previously toured with the band, and Torquay lass Sharon Whitbread, both of whom had been hired specifically for the one-off gig, arrived in Dubai at 3am on 31 December, spent the day sightseeing, performed to an 800-strong audience and were back in London at midnight on New Year's Day, £10,000 richer.

As Dave Mulvilhill quipped on the return journey from Dubai. 'How's that for Sheik, Rattle and Roll?'

The Midnight Blues

If, in the late 1950s the desire to succeed in the musical arena at semi-professional level had been directly relative to athleticism, the Olympic committee might well have elected to hold the next games upon Exmouth sea front, such was the enthusiasm, and drive of bands like The Midnight Blues.

David Green, Michael England, and John Lucas, long-time friends and pupils of Exmouth Grammar School, shared a passion for music, and in particular, traditional or 'trad' jazz. The prohibitive cost of brass and wind instruments put them out of reach, although Dave Green did realise one ambition when he joined Lympstone silver band, and was taught to play the trombone. The advent of skiffle, however, allowed the three teenagers to make music. Enter The Riversiders skiffle group (available for church fêtes, youth clubs etc., at reasonable rates, i.e. free).

In 1957, Mum and Dad Green had ordered – and Father Christmas had duly delivered – a Selmer Spanish guitar. David promptly learned the almost compulsory C, A minor, F and G7 chords and became rhythm guitarist and vocalist.

When Mike England acquired what most drummers would describe as a 'bit kit', and third musketeer John Lucas had scavenged a tea chest, broom handle and a sturdy length of 'hairy string', the group began to practise in earnest. Bob Parker and Dave's cousin John Ellis subsequently swelled the sound, on washboard and guitar respectively.

As the months passed, The Riversiders were actually beginning to sound like a group and, out of sheer bravado, they entered the widely advertised Six-Five Special skiffle contest, to be held at the Civic Hall in Exeter. The boys all thought that winning was as likely as Led Zeppelin being booked to play at a senior citizens' Christmas party, but to their joy and amazement, they performed well on the night and were placed third. In the interest of accuracy (and flag-waving by the author) it should be mentioned that The Duffels skiffle group from Tiverton came first. Hurrah!

L–R: Bruce, Howard, Dave

Although the three founding members thoroughly enjoyed playing skiffle, their love of trad jazz still existed. Throughout 1958, they regularly went to the Civic Hall to watch, admire, and learn from bands such as the Exmouth Jazzmen, occasionally having to walk the 10 miles or so home to Exmouth after missing the last train.

Life changed for Dave Green in 1962 when he met Bruce Miller. Lead

Dave and Bruce with drummer Stuart Clarke

guitarist Bruce had invited Dave to watch a group called The Royals rehearse. Striking up an instant friendship, it came as no surprise when, in January 1963, Bruce and Dave, together with drummer Howard Clarke, formed a rock band.

The Miller/Green combination named the new outfit The Midnight Blues. Their weekly practices, usually held in the nurses' recreation area of Exmouth Hospital, were both enjoyable and, as it transpired, worthwhile. The strong and flexible voices of Dave and Bruce enabled the trio to perform complex harmony numbers by The Hollies and The Beach Boys with apparent ease, and The Riversiders became a distant, though pleasant, memory.

Quite simply, the boys just 'clicked'. Over the next two years, The Midnight Blues steadily built a reputation for quality and presentation by using four

And Vince makes four

time-honoured maxims. Firstly, arrive at the venue in plenty of time, secondly, do your very best for the paying customers, thirdly, remember to say thank you at the end of the evening, and finally, practice makes pretty darned good, if perhaps not perfect.

The year 1965 saw a double change in the line-up. Drummer Howard Clarke wanted to pursue other musical avenues, and announced his intention to leave the band. He did, however, 'volunteer' a more than adequate replacement, in the shape of his brother Stuart. His suggestion was adopted, and Stuart became the Blues' sticks-man, staying with the trio until 1967.

The other change was the addition of bass player Vince Adey. Vince had been a member of the Newton Poppleford-based Scorpions rock band until their recent break-up, and had just relocated to Exmouth. On a chance visit to Exmouth Rugby Club, Vince was pleased to discover that a band called The Midnight Blues were performing that evening, and noted that the trio did not feature a bass player. Introducing himself during the interval, Vince commented on the fact and offered his services. As Dave and Bruce had already decided that the overall sound would be much improved with a bassist helping to drive the rhythm section, they invited the teenager to their next rehearsal. Left-handed Vince, younger brother of guitarist and keyboards man Peter, slotted in perfectly. The Midnight Blues now comprised the traditional lead, rhythm, bass guitar and drums format, with Dave and Bruce supplying the vocals.

The band went from strength to strength with Dave, Bruce and Vince remaining the constant constituents throughout the life of the Blues, an element essential to both semi-professional, and professional outfits. Vince did, in fact, leave the group for a short period, but was soon reunited with the two front men.

The 'Blues' at the Welcome Stranger Holiday Camp, Dawlish Warren

The nomadic tendencies of the drummers appeared to be the only stumbling block in an otherwise settled line-up. Drummer Stuart Clarke was replaced by Eddie Lomax in 1967. Eddie had left a trio called The Melotones, a family concern, as the other two members of the threesome were his mum and dad. A brilliant young drummer called Phillip Jones eventually took Eddie's position, although former drummer Howard Clarke returned briefly, and completed the jigsaw, remaining with The Midnight Blues throughout.

Regular rehearsals, and strict attention to the finer points of stage presentation brought the band to the notice of dance promoters, agents and club secretaries alike. Summer seasons at Sandy Bay, Exmouth, and the Welcome Stranger Holiday Camp across the Exe estuary in Dawlish Warren, were interspersed with a two nights' residency at the Tiverton Motel and sundry venues throughout Devon and, on occasions, Cornwall.

On one visit south of the Tamar The Midnight Blues encountered exotic dancer Miss Jojo Jago. The band had been booked to perform on the opening night of the Bodmin Jail Nightclub and were instructed to report to the club during the afternoon to take a band-call with Miss Jago.

By way of explanation, prior to the advent of cassette recorders, the 'band of the day' would be requested to provide the accompaniment for solo singers, dancers and the like, from the dots (sheet music) furnished by the latter. The rehearsal or familiarisation session with the non-instrumental singer or dancer is generally referred to as a band-call.

The pre-show band-call was extremely successful, Jojo suggestively but stylishly removing her clothes to the music provided by the Blues who insist they were far too busy committing the notes to memory to even notice.

That evening The Midnight Blues played supremely well. A large and appreciative audience gave the boys a rapturous welcome, and the dance

L–R: Dave, Phil Jones, Bruce

floor was full from the outset. The applause that the band received after virtually every number was as a whisper compared to the noise that heralded the arrival on stage of the seductive Miss Jago.

Dancing alluringly and casting off her already brief costume, Jojo concluded her act by whirling her brassiere around her head, then throwing it toward the wings. Perhaps the air-conditioning unit affected the trajectory, as it landed squarely across the neck of Vince's guitar. To his eternal credit, the bass player completed the number with little more than a smirk to match the unexpected trophy.

Dave Green, to this day, maintains that both his and Bruce's spectacles were also affected by the air-conditioning unit, and drummer Howard Clarke it is understood, played his kit sitting at such an obtuse angle merely because of an attack of cramp.

In later years, the band had a brief flirtation with a name change by adding the word New to The Midnight Blues but reverted to the original name, applying the 'If it's not broken, don't mend it' principle, and continued to delight audiences throughout the 1970s and 80s. In essence, the biographies in this book cover the years between 1954 and 1979, but it would be remiss not to mention that Dave Green, Vince Adey, and Phil Jones were still out there performing well into the 1990s. With Ray Heavens on lead guitar, the band was known as Outline 60.

PHOTO GALLERY

Actor Garfield Morgan with Gary Kane and the Tornadoes.

The In-Sect: (L–R) Tony Benellick, Dick Darlison, Bob Darlison, Terry Denning, Robin Phillips, Ray Beavis

The Chekkers: 'We were big in Cullompton!'

Hip Hooray Band: (L–R) John Snell, Brian Kirkby, Robin Phillips, Roger Pike, Grenville Downing; front left, Dave Mulvihill

The Starfires at St George's Hall, Exeter

Mark Shannon and the Sunsets at 400 Club, Torquay 1962

Dilendas Vaal: (L–R) Bob Ching, Graham Isaac, John Elliott, Ken Elliott

The Exonian Entertainment Co.

The Codiaks: (L–R) Graham Daniel, Alan Hart, Pete Evans, Robin Phillips

The Tuxedos: (L–R) Dave Parsons, Alan Bryant, Brian Nott, Colin Drake, Tommy Gibson

The Cougars with their road crew

77

The Tornadoes featured on the cover of South West Scene magazine.

The Corvettes

Four Steps Beyond at Exeter Castle before the tour in Germany: (L–R) Geoff Cox, Mike Emery, Colin Drake, Alan Bryant, Roger Walker

Combined advertisement and ticket from an Axminster newspaper in 1958

The Mustangs outside Bedford Street Post Office, Exeter: (L–R) Geoff Cox, Chris Lamacraft, Johnny Cordell, Dave Cox, Dave Vincent

The Harmonica Blackjacks: (L–R) Ted Greenham, George Bowker, Tony Smythe, Pete Cummins, Peter Tolliday

Atlantis

Dance Scene

Corvettes onstage at the ABC Theatre 1963: (L–R) John Greenslade, Dave Smale, Len Simpson, Percy Turner

Dave Smale: 'Chiefy told me to hit the flaming thing'

The Bluesounds

The Guild: Back (L–R), Stuart Boyles, Mike Vaughan-Jones, Stuart Howe; front (L–R), Kenny Strange, Terry Denning

The Groups

PART TWO

L–R: Chris Lamacraft,
Dave Vincent, Dave Cox,
John Orton, Geoff Cox

The Mustangs

This second band to hail from suburbia featured five young men of similar age and disposition who were all members of the youth club held at Pinhoe Middle School in Harrington Lane, and who acquired the name of their beat group from a cuddly toy. Farmer's son David Vincent, and Boys' Brigade drummer David Cox, together with their friends Tony Frood, Christopher Lamacraft and Geoffrey Stamp, formed The Mustangs in 1958.

Pinhoe Youth Club, The Mustangs' very first gig. OK, So where's the goat?

The furry toy in question was in fact a goat. It had been 'abandoned' at the Youth Club and remained unclaimed. Adopted by the band as its mascot, it was ceremoniously placed at the foot of the bass drum at the start of each practice session. When someone politely queried the breed of the animal, Dave Cox – with the customary acerbic wit and sarcasm of drummers – replied, 'It's a flaming mustang isn't it!'

The usual venue for rehearsals was Monkerton Farm, home of the Vincent family, normally a tranquil oasis in the heart of the Devonshire countryside, unless of course it happened to be a Wednesday – practice nights for The Mustangs. The band comprised three guitarists, each with an electric guitar, small practice amplifier and very little musical knowledge, a drummer – who was more accustomed to vying with two dozen bugles for audibility – and a trainee sax-ophonist/vocalist who also shouldered the managerial responsibilities.

By the winter of 1958, they had mastered sufficient material to to provide an evening of entertainment at the local youth club. Dave's brother Colin, and Mr Stamp Snr were seconded to drive a brace of Austin 16s, one of which belonged to the latter, the other to Albert Vincent, Dave's father. Along with with Dave Cox's Ford Anglia, they easily conveyed the Mustang's gear to Harrington Lane.

The Mustangs' debut at the 400 Club, Torquay

Lead guitarist Tony Frood, rhythm guitarist Geoff Stamp, and bass player Chris Lamacraft had pooled their limited finances, and purchased a Vox AC30 amplifier, into which all three guitars were plugged, Dave Vincent sang lustily through a 10-watt output practice amp, and Dave Cox orchestrated the whole thing splendidly.

The Mustangs' debut public performance was an unqualified success. This was partially attributable to the countless hours of rehearsal, and largely due to the durability, and good old British workmanship employed in the manufacture of Vox amplifiers. Invitations to play at other youth clubs in the surrounding area followed, and the band 'had arrived'.

The year 1958 was also the one in which three of the lads left school. Chris

Lamacraft secured an apprenticeship with SWEB (the South Western Electricity Board) and Geoff Stamp entered the building trade with a company called Woodman, appropriately as an apprenticed carpenter. Dave Vincent moved from broilers to boilers when he joined Whippell & Row. Initially, this meant working on the shop-floor learning about domestic and industrial heating systems, after which he was to be transferred to the drawing office. Tony Frood and Dave Cox, being a few months older, were already employed as engineers, with British Rail and Exeter Aircraft respectively.

During the next twelve months, the boys strove to develop their play-list and stage presentation. Dave Vincent adopted the stage name Dave Lane and continued to receive saxophone lessons from John Glanfield who, as well as being music teacher at Broadclyst Community College, could regularly be seen fronting his own band, The Stars.

Dave's first saxophone, bought in 1960 from Bill Greenhalgh's, gave The Mustangs a distinct edge. Prior to the onset of the swinging 60s, the saxophone had primarily been featured with dance bands and orchestras, and therefore, when imaginatively used in a rock and roll outfit, was something of a novelty.

Dave Lane was now triple-hatted as manager, vocalist, and sax player, and appeared to experience only minor difficulties in combining those roles. As a manager, he thought he was doing OK. He had a desk diary, and a penchant for pulling booking fees from the air. Each of the guitarists now possessed a Vox amplifier, and he himself now sang through a new public address system. Dave Cox would be seen at the next gig sitting proudly behind a new Trixon drum-kit, and he had personally stumped-up the cash to purchase an Austin 'J' range van, which would enable musicians, equipment and girlfriends to arrive at a venue simultaneously.

The band was signed to LMD Entertainment's of Torquay at the end of 1960, and with the increased volume of work came increased popularity. Audiences throughout Devon and Cornwall loved the five-piece sound, and the same faces would often be seen at dances many miles distant. In one particularly busy week, the band performed at Okehampton Town Hall, the Winter Gardens in Newquay and the Flamingo Club in Redruth, where they shared the bill with Eric Burdon and The Animals, and for which they received a fee of £35.

In January 1963, Dave Lane donned his manager's hat, and announced his intention to try to recruit a vocalist. This would allow him to retire to the far reaches of the stage, where he could concentrate solely on his sax playing. He added that, as the band was now fully booked for the whole of the year, at an average of six bookings each week, they should seriously consider the professional option.

The Mustangs were fortunate indeed to enlist the services of a first-rate vocalist. Born in Exeter, educated at Ladysmith School and formerly with The Harlequins, John Orton had been pleased to an accept invitation to front the band, having longed to be a part of an outfit with a professional outlook for some time. Agent Lionel Digby gave John the stage name Cordell on the basis that all top acts were identified by their front man – Cliff Richard and The Shadows, Gerry and The Pacemakers etc. His suggestion was taken on board, and the band became Johnny Cordell and the Mustangs.

The decision to turn professional was finally made in July 1964, except for Geoff Stamp and Tony Frood who, after lengthy discussions with their families and much soul-searching, declined to take the gamble and ended their six years' association with the band.

There was but one replacement for Geoff Stamp and Tony. Geoff Cox, whose name would have served as a permanent reminder of both past and present members of the group had he not taken the stage name Geoff Adams, joined The Mustangs as both lead and rhythm guitarist. Earlier in the year, band leader Dave had far-sightedly purchased an electric organ, learned to play the more commonly used chords and was now able to swap lead, rhythm and vocal harmony duties with Geoff, further adding to the band's versatility.

Summer vacations were taken as and when the boys' busy schedule allowed. A cancellation due to a fire at a venue in Torquay, permitted Dave Lane to accept an offer from the Jayvee Entertainment's Agency in Swansea for The Mustangs to appear at the Miners' Welfare Club in a village called Pentreclwydau, Wales. 'If you get stuck bach,' the agent had said to Dave, 'give me a ring and I'll direct you, isn't it.'

Having performed in venues throughout Devon and Cornwall, the five adolescents who had never ventured north of Bristol, now had to find a social club in a village somewhere in the South of Wales, the name of which as fluent Devonian speaking musicians, none of them could pronounce, or find in their AA atlas. Dave Lane remembers that he made three or four telephone calls to Jayvee after crossing the Severn Bridge, and stopped as

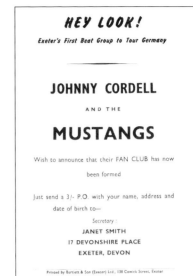

As worn by The Beatles

many times to ask for directions, by pointing to the name of the village on the contract. They finally decided to drive to the agency office in Swansea and were flabbergasted to find on their arrival that it had closed for the day. Commendably, The Mustangs reached the little village in the Vale of Neath, took stock of the fact that the street, shop windows and vehicles were covered in a fine black dust, found the social club, and treated the miners, their families and guests to a wonderful evening.

Packing up afterwards, Dave Lane was asked by a member of the club committee where the band was staying overnight. When he heard that they would be snuggling down in their 'luxurious' Bedford Dormobile, he was horrified. Within minutes, he had arranged overnight accommodation for the lads, billeting them with other club members. John Orton recalls that he and Dave Lane stayed with a Mr and Mrs Murphy, a miner, and the local midwife.

A telegram from Lionel Digby awaited their return. The boss of LMD Entertainment's had contracted The Mustangs to a four-month tour in Germany, playing the Star Palast clubs in Bremen, Kiel and Hamburg as part of a four-outfit tour. On 26 August 1964 the boys stood on the quayside, in the shadow of the white cliffs at Dover, as their van was hoisted aboard the ship that would take them to Rotterdam. There they would spend a couple of days sightseeing, before travelling on to Bremen and their opening night, Monday 1 September.

On the balcony of the Star Palast Club, Bremen

On arrival at the club in Bremen, The Mustangs were introduced to the other three bands: from Liverpool, The Exchequers and The Undertakers, a band that was to become extremely well known, and an outfit from Bath whose name has unfortunately slipped from the memory. Chatting with the lead

guitarist of The Undertakers later that day, Geoff Cox mentioned that he had not seen their van in the car park. 'Oh yeah well, replied the guitarist, we *flew* in this morning and our roadies should be here with the van and the kit tonight.'

The Undertakers were to hit the headlines later that year for all the wrong reasons. Whilst in Germany they planned to visit Berlin and apply some tasteful graffiti to the famous wall: 'Val Doonican is a pilchard' for instance, or 'Cliff Richard is rubbish', as a publicity stunt. Armed with brushes and paint, The Undertakers were arrested by the police before they could reach the notorious landmark.

The Mustangs quickly became accustomed to their new hours of work. Star Palast Clubs opened at 4pm and closed at 4am. In a six-day working week over a four-week period, each of the four bands would play for one hour then rest for three hours throughout the twelve-hour shift, with the order of appearance rotated weekly. At the end of each four-week cycle, the tour would move to the next club listed on the itinerary. The Mustangs left Bremen for Kiel at the end of September, having been paid for three and a half weeks' work only. Short payment was also made on completion of the band's stints in both Kiel and Hamburg.

Dave Lane recollects that the clubs were very pleasant places in which to play and with an average daily 'gate' of approximately 3000, very well supported. 'Unfortunately for us, they could never seem to get our money right, and basically we just got fed up with the whole deal and came home.'

The original line-up plus Johnny Cordell

The Mustangs split at the end of 1964, with Geoff Cox joining Exeter band Four Steps Beyond. His namesake, drummer Dave Cox, and vocalist John Orton teamed up with guitar ace Brian Wright and John Phripp in forming a truly sensational vocal harmony band called The Variations. (See *Oh No! It's Local Rock and Roll …but I like it* – Mid Devon volume.)

Sue Binmore, destined to become Mrs Lamacraft, had given her boyfriend, bass player Chris, her total support throughout his playing days, but perhaps understandably was not too disappointed when he relinquished his musical career in favour of a steady job.

Dave Vincent became the manager of The Variations, a position he held for a period of eighteen months before handing over to his good friend John Carr. John had been The Variations' road manager from the outset, and was held in the highest regard by all that knew him.

Pure Gold formerly The Pioneers

Apprentice Marine Engineering Officer Bob Jarvis, known to all as BJ, had joined the Merchant Navy in 1959. Born and educated in Exmouth, he had attended an interview at the offices of the Federal Steam Navigation Company, allied to the New Zealand Shipping Company in Leadenhall Street, London, and had signed-on for a five-year period, four of which were to be spent afloat.

Four years passed quickly enough. Trips to Australia, New Zealand, Singapore, and the USA were interspersed with 'hops' across the channel to Hamburg and Rotterdam, and the cadets were granted three weeks' leave after each completed six-monthly trip.

Laden with cash, there being little to buy onboard ship, Bob spent his first week's leave at his parent's new home in Exeter, and his first month's wages at Bill Greenhalgh's music emporium. He bought a Hofner Club '60' guitar complete with a Bigsby tremolo arm, and a Truvoice 10-watt amplifier. Formerly a member of The Bandits skiffle group, and with a deep-seated love of music, Bob whiled away the remaining fortnight in the company of fellow shipmate James 'Jim' Boughey (pronounced Bowie – like the knife). Jim lived with his parents in Wallasey, just across the Mersey from Liverpool, and his

Officers and cadets of the MV Otaio in Liverpool 1960: Bob Jarvis, middle row third left; Jim Boughey, second row from back, sixth right

father managed a warehouse in Matthew Street, beneath which was the Cavern Club.

Bob and Jim's excursion to the Cavern proved to be memorable. It was Bob's birthday, and the pair had consumed several pints of good old Lancashire ale before catching the ferry – soon to be brought to the attention of millions by Gerry Marsden, which would take them across the Mersey. A slothful stagger eventually brought them to Matthew Street and the Cavern. A local group called The Beatles was on stage, and BJ decided that he would ask them to sing his favourite song as a sort of personal birthday gift. Approaching the small dais from the right, BJ stood to the side, amidst a pile of guitar and drum cases, and waited for the band to finish what they were playing.

'It's my birthday today, could you play "Memphis Tennessee" for me?' he asked.

John Lennon's reply suggested that he was hot, under a great deal of stress, and perhaps subconsciously thinking about the release of the band's first record, a song he had co-written with bass guitarist Paul McCartney called 'Love Me Do'.

BJ took only seconds to carry out John's instructions to rearrange the words Off Sod into a well-known phrase or saying. Walking to the other side of the stage, he repeated his request to Paul. Some ten minutes later, George Harrison announced to the heaving masses that it was Bob's birthday, and his wish was granted.

Jim and BJ often hitchhiked from their respective homes to London. Meeting at a pre-arranged location, they regularly visited The Marquee in Wardour Street, the Bag O' Nails, and the nearby '100' Club, to listen to the likes of Long John Baldry, John Mayall's Bluesbreakers, at the time featuring a guitarist called Eric Clapton, the Graham Bond Organisation and Manfred Mann.

In the fifth and final year of their apprenticeship, BJ and Jim became landlocked in Scotland, Bob working for the Kincade company in Greenock who manufactured ships' engines, and his pal Jim similarly employed with a shipbuilding company further up the Clyde.

Cadet Officer Robert Jarvis

The two apprentices, whilst missing the three weeks' leave bi-annually, frequently met at the appropriately named All-Nighter Club in Glasgow. BJ became an avid fan of Alex Harvey on his first visit there. Alex and his band had recently returned from Hamburg where they had just cut their latest LP and were celebrating its release with the Glasgow gig. BJ ordered the vinyl record that same morning; the album is still in his record collection and he remains an ardent supporter of the SAHB, the Sensational Alex Harvey Band.

Jim Boughey and Bob Jarvis qualified as naval engineering officers in the summer of 1964, and the author is reliably informed that both officers passed out twice during the day of presentation. Sadly, Bob and his pal lost contact shortly after qualifying.

BJ spent the next few months on cargo vessels prior to becoming the seventh officer on an oil tanker. Life aboard the tanker became wearisome very quickly. BJ recalls, 'We would steam to the oil terminal at Mina Al Ahmadi in Kuwait, at which there was nothing more than a little water and a lot of sand, fill up, which would take about a day and a half, and then steam back to Rotterdam. Now is that boring or what?'

Bob left the Merchant Navy at the end of 1964 suffering from what he describes as terminal tedium. Remembering the happy times that he had spent in Glasgow, he resolved to seek accommodation and employment there.

He found lodgings in the home of a recently divorced man called John 'Jock' McDermott who lived in Govan Road, some 300 yards from the Gorbals. Reporting to a seedy tenement block for an interview after answering an advertisement in the local newspaper for an area sales representative, BJ was surprised to find that he was the only applicant, and astounded when he was hired almost immediately. All became clear when he realised he would be selling encyclopaedias door to door. He endured three days of rejection, insults and threats before common sense superseded valour.

Week two saw him bravely attempting to purvey Drapery (curtains, clothes and bedding) to the same customer base. Week three was spent applying for jobs and attending high-level lunchtime discussions at Jock's local. Within six weeks of his return to Glasgow, BJ had a job with the Singer Sewing Machine Company, as a clerk in their work study department, a job which he liked, but this too was short-lived. After a Christmas visit visit home, Bob returned to be told he was fired. After clearing his desk Bob decided it was time to return to Devon.

Back in the South West and after a spell of self-employment, he acquired a position with Centrax, based in Shaldon Road at Newton Abbot, who specialised in gas-turbine-driven equipment. Before long fellow worker Gordon Hickman, a guitar-playing engineer, had heard that BJ also played the guitar and asked him if would like to form a band.

Photocall: (L–R) Glyn Evans, Gordon Hickman, Bob Jarvis

BJ joined Gordon and a young guitarist called Glyn Evans in founding a country and western trio named The Pioneers. Glyn, a friend of Gordon and the possessor of a fine singing voice, had gained some experience by singing and strumming along with his piano-playing mum at her regular Saturday night booking in a pub in the Exwick area of Exeter. Practices were held at Gordon's house in Belmont Terrace, and the trio played at youth clubs and public houses throughout Exeter.

BJ had constructed a speaker cabinet from some offcuts of oak, procured by Gordon from a colleague at Centrax who assisted in the manufacture of coffins in his leisure time Having decided to convert his six-string Hofner guitar to a bass, BJ removed the now redundant Bigsby tremolo arm, and swapped the article with Gordon in exchange for a 15in bass speaker. The little Hofner Club '60' was fitted with bass strings, and The Pioneers had a bass guitarist.

The trio enjoyed a little success during the first eighteen months, but both Glyn and BJ grew tired of playing songs with lyrics capable of making the happiest of people feel positively suicidal, and suggested that the trio bring rock and roll into the act. Gordon was totally averse to the idea and voiced his opinion clearly. Unable to accept this intransigence, Glyn and BJ left The Pioneers to form their own band.

Pure Gold was born at the start of 1969. Eagle-eyed BJ had spotted a cigarette packet bearing the logo Pure Gold in the gutter and thought that the name was suitable for a group. Glyn agreed but with reservations. 'It's a brand name he said, we'll have to get permission to use it.' A letter was sent to Gallaher, requesting permission to use the words Pure Gold. A prompt reply from a Mr Place in the marketing department assured the lads that the words carried no copyright and together with the company's best wishes for the band's future enclosed a packet of twenty Pure Gold cigarettes.

The letter from Benson & Hedges, dated 10 April 1969

Accomplished guitarist John West, forcibly reminded by BJ that they were after all related (John's great-grandfather and BJ's great-grandmother were brother and sister), joined Pure Gold as the lead guitarist. Born in 1948, John's interest in music began at the age of four with a harmonica. Progressing to a plastic ukulele, which he accidentally sat on, to be replaced with a wooden one, it soon became obvious that he was going to be a very good musician. Living in Sampford Peverell, he took informal guitar lessons with a boy named Bruce Thomas whose parents ran a guest-house near the canal on the outskirts of the village, and within weeks the pupil was instructing the master. Peter Pengelly, a friend at Sampford Peverell Primary School teamed up with Bruce and John in forming a little hobby band, playing in public for the first time in 1962, at a Christmas concert in the village hall.

Around 1964, John's parents moved to Exeter and he wasted little time in joining a group, becoming a member of The Chordettes, his first real band. They comprised John playing lead guitar, a bass guitarist called Barry who was supplanted by Ian 'Bud' Street, rhythm guitarist Derek Holmes, vocalist Roger Richards, and drummer Mike Ewings. Mike's father Bob was the group's manager.

The Chordettes were mildly successful. One of the first cities to be 'twinned', Exeter City Council and the twinning committee put together a massive package for a visit to Rennes in France – one of the gifts is thought to have

At Taunton Labour Club: (L–R) John West, Glyn Evans, Bob Jarvis

been a double-decker bus. Invited to represent Exeter, the Chordettes played 13 gigs in seven days, which included appearances on French radio and television networks.

When the Chordettes eventually folded, John played with an outfit called Intercity Sounds, which featured Terry Greenslade (brother of ESR boss John), Bob Kilroy, and Mike Vanstone. The band was short-lived and disbanded after only twelve months and John enjoyed a brief respite before receiving the aforementioned call-up from Bob Jarvis. Musicians of John West's calibre normally have little need or inclination to rehearse, and it was very much a case of, 'What key is it in? OK – a one-two-three-four.'

Pure Gold had been plying their trade on the local scene for almost a year when BJ began to have a few personal problems, which made the task of running a band difficult, he and his girlfriend having recently moved into a flat that had no telephone and needed a great deal of refurbishment. BJ ruefully left the trio in the autumn of 1969. John and Glyn continued to perform as Pure Gold for a month or two following Bob's departure but finally decided to pack it in. BJ proved to himself (and his girlfriend) that his skills lay in music rather than home renovation, and after a brief spell with The Red Aces dance band joined the very popular Hotspots.

John West was invited to join Alan Hempstead's Sounds Tijuana, the rhythm section of which – John, Dale Hooper, Mike Emery and Jim Newton – evolved into Haze. Returning to his country roots, Glyn Evan's vocal dexterity and accurate guitar playing found him employment with John Forsey and steel guitar player Richard Harris in Stringband.

Sounds Tijuana, featuring Alan and Judy Hempstead, Mike Emery, John West, Jim Newton

The Rejects, and The Vic Palmer Combo

Ask any musician and you are sure to be told that there was one particular song or tune that 'kick-started' his or her musical career.

Lonnie Donegan's 'Rock Island Line' did it for Vic Palmer. The classic skiffle number, Donegan's first chart entry from January 1956, inspired the youngster to start saving a shilling or two a week towards buying his first guitar. Having eventually raised the money, Vic headed for Bernie Chinn's shop (now Bill Greenhalgh's) in Fore Street, emerging two hours later with a round-holed Spanish guitar for the princely sum of £4.15s.0d. (£4.75p).

Together with some of his friends, also budding guitarists, at St Luke's senior school, which became the Vincent Thompson School and is now St Luke's High School, he learned the basic chord shapes required to strum along to many of the skiffle favourites of the time. Vic's other great passion was football; he was regularly selected to play for the Exeter City Colts team, and captained Devon's Youth, but despite these schoolboy honours his first love remained the music.

He became a member of The City Ramblers skiffle group at the invitation of Colin Smythe. A pupil at John Stocker School, he had formed the little group at the Emmanuel Youth Club with David Halford, John Cullum and Barry Chalk.

Rivalry was rife in the Smythe household, in that Colin's brother Tony was a guitarist with The Redhills skiffle group. As the name suggests, all six members of the band – Tony Madge, Gordon Clark, Len Burgess, Albert White, Alfie Richardson, and of course Tony – lived in the Redhills area of the city. Drummer Alfie worked at Willeys in Haven Road, whose management granted the group permission to use the staff club for rehearsal.

There were many reasons why The Redhills skiffle group broke up, not the least of which was the call-up for National Service of several of its members, and Tony Smythe and Alfie Richardson joined The City Ramblers playing rhythm guitar and drums respectively.

Colin and Tony Smythe at the Co-op Hall, Torquay

Vic Palmer's boundless enthusiasm was infectious and shared by the other 'Ramblers', guitar-playing brothers Tony and Colin Smythe who was also the group's vocalist, tea-chest bassist Barry Chalk, drummer Alfie Richardson and yet another plectrum wielder, called Ray.

Growing in confidence and repertoire, the group felt ably equipped to accept the occasional booking, and subsequently became regular and popular performers at Willeys' Club in addition to many other local venues. Vic always felt, however, that his Spanish guitar was just not loud enough.

He solved the problem with an earpiece, taken from a pair of pre-war military headphones, some bits of Meccano, and a couple of screws. Incredibly, and much to the annoyance of his parents Ted and Joyce, this primitive attachment, when connected to the rear of their radiogram, actually worked.

Continental Coffee Bar,
Exmouth

With the 'stage-struck' bit firmly in their mouths, the compulsory moody look, and an air of determination, The City Ramblers entered a local entertainment contest held at the Gaumont cinema in North Street Exeter, and achieved second place. Vic cannot remember what song the 'Ramblers' performed that day, but does recall that the winning act gave a stylish rendition of 'Green Back Dollar'.

School days ended and in 1958, although Vic and Tony Smythe were to take the stage together again with Gary Kane's Tornadoes, The City Ramblers went their separate ways.

Vic worked in the spare parts department of Pike's garage earning £1.10s. (£1.50p) net per week. But by saving steadily, as for his first instrument, Vic managed to raise the £20 necessary to buy his next guitar, a Hoyer, twin pick-up archtop. It was during this period that he began to develop an interest in the piano. Largely self-taught by 'tinkering and watching', Vic had mastered several tunes by the time that Gary Kane invited him to join The Tornadoes as their lead guitarist.

His complete transition to the organ resulted from a dance at the great hall on the campus of Exeter University. The Tornadoes were the support act to The Graham Bond Organisation, a professional outfit featuring band leader

At the Regal, Exmouth: (L–R)
Dean Hunter (Tony Smythe);
Danny Ocean (Alan Maggs);
Gary Kane (Mike Parr);
Tony London (Tony Harper);
Vic Diamond (Vic Palmer)

Graham Bond on organ and alto saxophone, Dick Heckstall-Smith on tenor sax, Jack Bruce on bass guitar, and Ginger Baker on drums.

Vic was smitten with the myriad of sounds that Bond was getting from his Hammond organ and Leslie rotary speaker, and ordered an identical combination the very next day from Minns Music in Paris Street, at a cost of £630. He left The Tornadoes shortly after, his place being taken by John Greenslade, and did not play the guitar again.

For a brief period he teamed up with a band from Newton Abbot led by skilful guitarist Derek Luscombe, but longed to form his own band. His wish became reality with assistance from three former Tornadoes. Drummer Tony Harper, bass player Alan Maggs, and rhythm guitarist Tony Smythe, teamed with Vic in the founding of a new group. The band, however, did not have a name!

The situation was resolved by a group of Exeter University students who after seeing a film about university life called 'The Wild and the Willing' decided to make their own true-to-life version which was to be called The Rejects. Vic was asked by an acquaintance, a science student called Miles, if he and

The Combo at the Fisherman's Cot, Bickleigh.

the boys would both compose, and perform the film score. Both tasks were successfully accomplished, and the band adopted the title of the film.

In the short time that The Rejects were a 'going concern', about twelve months or so, there were two noteworthy occurrences. Firstly, Mike Emery replaced rhythm guitarist Tony Smythe, and secondly, Vic Palmer became a DIY legend.

Booked to play at the Athena Club in New North Road, Exeter, The Rejects arrived at the venue and began to unload the Commer van, a recent purchase from Mike Emery's garage-owning father, and to their horror discovered that Vic's Hammond organ was substantially wider than the doorway.

The general air of bemusement turned to disbelief as Vic produced a crosscut handsaw from the back of the van, manhandled the instrument into a vertical position and proceeded to cut the expensive organ in half. The two halves were carried up to the first-floor club, reassembled, and apparently sounded as good as it ever did.

When The Rejects disbanded, Vic rejoined Derek Luscombe's outfit for a while prior to becoming the organist with The Maurice Price Band. Maurice had approached Vic at the Embassy ballroom (later to be named the Caprice Club – situated below the Rougemont Hotel in Queen Street) where Derek's band played each Saturday, and told him, one, that he needed an organist, and two, that regular work awaited. Vic discussed the proposition with Derek, and later accepted Maurice's offer.

The eventual break with Maurice Price was amicable enough, and largely stemmed from Vic's desire to 'captain his own ship'. The Vic Palmer Combo initially comprised lead guitarist Ray Hill, drummer Ronnie Graham, bass player Stuart Boyles, vocalist Tony Osborne and band leader and organist Vic.

The sound was often augmented with brass and or woodwind. Formerly with the Welsh Philharmonic Orchestra, clarinettist and tenor-saxophonist Alan Lewis, trumpet players Don Brooks and Bill Smith, and the hugely

Westward Ho! Holiday Camp, 1970

talented Ron 'If it's got a reed I'll get a tune out of it' Ginger, all lent their considerable musical weight to the combo when called upon.

The dexterity and quality of the combo gained them a three-night's residency at the Fisherman's Cot, Bickleigh. The riverside pub in the beautiful Exe Valley between Tiverton and Exeter is allegedly where Paul Simon derived the inspiration to compose his classic song 'Bridge Over Troubled Water.' After several years at the Cot, Vic decided that the band needed 'a change of scenery', and the combo took up a bi-monthly booking at the Shrubbery in Ilminster, Somerset, allowing them to do local gigs at weekends.

After the move from the Fisherman's Cot, there were gradual changes in the combo's line-up. Ray Hill decided to focus his skills on the pedal steel guitar and joined John Forsey's Stringband. Tony Osborne yielded to pressure from outside sources and rejoined Maurice Price, his place in the Combo being taken by Mike O'Connor, formerly the vocalist with The Hotspots and The Silvertones. The brilliant Ronnie Graham headed northward to Tiverton to link up with his old friend Ginger Walker. Formerly London-based, Paul Hiley and the outstanding Dave Tolby both drummed with the band prior to January 1977 when Vic was fortunate to acquire the services of Tiverton's top rock drummer Geoff Bulley.

The single other important change to the new-look combo was the enlistment of teenage vocalist and guitarist Andy Ford. It was evident that the multi-talented youngster had the drive and ambition to succeed in the music business, and it came as no surprise to Vic, Stuart or Geoff when he turned professional and launched his solo career.

The Combo, now reduced to a trio (Mike O'Connor had left the band shortly after Andy's arrival), continued to delight audiences countywide with Vic shouldering the responsibility for vocals.

Sadly, Stuart Boyles died in September 1980. Vic Palmer had been holidaying on the Norfolk Broads with family and friends when a police launch pulled alongside their rented houseboat. Vic was asked to contact his daughter urgently and was told of Stuart's death. All bookings were immediately cancelled. Friend, and former drummer with the Combo, Ronnie Graham relayed the news to a stunned Geoff Bulley who was packed and ready to leave for a holiday in Spain later that same day.

Ronnie Graham at the BBC Studios, Plymouth

But, as they say, life goes on, and Vic and Geoff eventually felt able to face public performances again. John West, nominally a lead guitarist and well respected as such, stood in on bass guitar until the recruitment of Peter Hunt.

Certainly one of the finest bass guitarists ever to grace the county's stages, Peter, from Wellington in Somerset, occasionally played under the name Pete Maxwell in deference to his father who was Musical Director of the Princess Theatre Orchestra in Torquay.

The trio, playing as The Vic Palmer Sound, continued to provide top-quality entertainment for the next two years. Ultimately, the economic climate convinced Vic that to go solo was his only option. The band's final gig was at the Centre Spot Club in Exeter on 31 December 1982.

At the time of writing, the 'two-piece' Hammond organ has long since been replaced by a sleek Japanese keyboard which Vic plays merely for his own enjoyment. The author suspects, however, that among the thousands of voices available to the user of the aforementioned keyboard, there is one that sounds suspiciously like a Hammond.

♪ ♫ ♪

The Royals incorporating The Graduates, and The Law

It is probably helpful to explain here that friendly, but intense rivalry existed between The Royals and The Graduates, but in the following years a merging of the two outfits produced a band called The Law.

In both this book and its predecessor a dedication has been included to the parents of all the musicians mentioned. Albert Collins took the duties of a parent to another level by offering to become the manager of The Royals.

Bert's eldest son Terry, the lead guitarist and makeshift drummer of the Exmouth-based outfit, had co-founded the band towards the end of the 1950s, with school friends Mike 'Ferdy' Watts, Keith Heaton, and vocalist and official drummer Kenny Pynn.

Terry and Keith regularly practised during their lunch break at Exmouth Secondary Modern School, and would then hold a full rehearsal in the front room of the Collins household. With Bert's wife Jean providing coffee and sandwiches, all agreed it was a great place in which to make music.

Terry's brother Michael, always known as Mick and two years his junior, loved music and dearly wished to have a go at playing the drums. Unfortunately, he was an extremely shy boy and far too nervous to ask, and secondly, he was invariably told to 'Bog Off' during practice sessions.

Slowly but surely, the group began to build a library of instrumentals and vocals. Terry Collins appeared to have little difficulty in playing tunes by The Shadows and The Ventures, and Kenny Pynn enjoyed his attempts to emulate Gene Vincent, Little Richard and Ray Charles.

Jean & Bert Collins' front room

Listening to the band rehearsing one evening, Bert Collins considered the implications of managing a beat group. On the credit side, the lads sounded reasonably good and were not lacking in confidence. On the debit side, they were young, had no transport and needed new instruments, microphones, and amplification; they knew nothing about stage presentation and had never given a public performance; finally, they had about three shillings (15p) between them.

'Would you like me to manage the group?' asked Bert?

A coach driver with Greenslade's Tours, Bert Collins was a good-natured, gregarious character with a generally optimistic outlook on life. He possessed a good local topographical knowledge, and was well known and respected in the community. Being also a monarchist and fiercely patriotic, accordingly the band was named The Royals.

Bert insisted that The Royals did not question his decisions and that they follow a strict code of conduct at all times. In return, he would provide the means to acquire new instruments, amplification and stage wear, which was to be kept spotlessly clean, and worn only when performing.

Bert Collins with his company vehicle

With their new equipment and costumes duly acquired, the young musicians threw themselves into rehearsals with a new intensity and dedication. Tonal quality, phrasing, and variance of volume became a matter of importance, and the improvement in both the music and the presentation was obvious even to the untrained ear.

Initially playing in local youth and social clubs, The Royals were soon to be seen at venues, not only in the immediate locale, but also in Exeter and throughout East Devon.

When vocalist and drummer Kenny Pynn left the band to get married The Royals suddenly had a dual problem. Kenny had been the band's vocalist and drummer, and his departure meant the enlistment of at least one, but probably two, musicians. The son of a local butcher, and coincidentally sharing the same Christian name, Kenny Strange was recruited as the band's

Photocall at Exmouth Pavilion with fourteen-year-old drummer Mick Collins

Exmouth Pavillion minus one rhythm guitarist

singer. A distant relative of the Collins family, Dennis Carpenter, became the new drummer thereby restoring the outfit to its usual line-up. His wife Kay, stage name Kay Lee, joined The Royals as a vocalist for a short time but left, along with her drummer husband, shortly afterwards.

Auditions were held to find a new drummer. The successful applicant, owner of an immaculate set of Trixon drums and whose name is another that has slipped from the memory, stored his drums at the Collins' house. Whilst playing truant from school one day, naughty Mick Collins seized the opportunity to realise his ambition of becoming a drummer.

'Mick, what the devil are you doing, why aren't you at school?' his mother's voice rang out.
'Oh hello Mum, I didn't feel very well, and they sent me home.'
'If you're feeling poorly, you should be in bed, so move it!'
'Yes Mum.'

Mick had at last played the drums for the first time and it had felt great. His next goal was to play on a real stage with a proper band like The Royals. The only cloud was that he would doubtless get a walloping from his dad. In fact, although he did receive a ticking-off from his father, Bert now realised just how desperate Mick was to become an entertainer like his elder brother.

He was to get his chance much sooner than he had anticipated. Bert had arranged for a professional photographer to take a series of publicity shots, but the new drummer failed to turn up. An exasperated Bert said, 'Mick, sit behind the drums and try not to look too stupid.' The speed at which young Mick moved into position near scorched the shag pile. The evidently camera-shy owner of the drum-kit also failed to attend the next two practice sessions, and was sacked by an irate Royals manager soon after.

The sacking did, however, create a major problem for the band. The Royals were booked to appear at Dartmoor Prison to entertain the prison officers, their wives, and ancillary staff in three days' time, and they had no drummer. Terry Collins suggested that Mick be offered the job but the general consensus was that he was too young, and that an experienced drummer must be found, and quickly!

Loading the band wagon:
(L–R) Maureen's friend,
Maureen Woodward née
Collins, Dapper, Terry Collins

Despite the efforts of Bert and the boys, the day of the engagement at Dartmoor Prison came and a suitable drummer had still not been found. The Royals were left without options and Mick was about to be thrown in at the deep end, wearing a hastily doctored spare pair of stage trousers belonging to Keith Heaton. He sold his Spanish guitar for £4.10s.0d. (£4.50p) to acquire the deposit for a small Ajax drum-kit, and after collecting it from Exeter, it was off to the gig.

The Royals played well and managed to disguise several loose starts and endings. Mick was a study in concentration throughout the evening, doing his very best not to let brother 'Bunky' (Terry's nickname) and the rest of the band down. Mick is quoted as being, politely translated, 'frightfully nervous' all night. But the boys were impressed with his overall performance, and informed him that he now had the job on a permanent basis. He practised daily, much to the annoyance of the neighbours, and gradually became a very skilled drummer.

The Royals, now with an apparently settled line-up, were an extremely busy outfit, and appeared at venues from Chard to Callington, and Tiverton to Tintagel.

At the beginning of 1962 Stan Strange, the father of vocalist Kenny, bought a butchery business in Cullompton near Tiverton, and moved to Plymtree with his wife and family. Kenny found that the additional travelling between Exmouth and his new home at the end of every booking and on rehearsal nights was becoming a drag, and amicably parted company with The Royals later that year. Kenny subsequently fronted Tiverton outfit The Starfires, founded by John 'Ginger' Walker and his brother Dave.

Kenny Pynn rejoined The Royals as lead vocalist, happy in the knowledge that he would not be required to perform the dual roles of lead singer and drummer, as he had done in his first spell with the band.

It is said that familiarity breeds contempt, and one cannot help wondering whether it was the family connection of Bunky and Mick, the business pressures encountered by Keith Heaton and 'Ferdy' Watts, or the personal problems that seemed to haunt Kenny Pynn, that triggered the break-up of The Royals.

Performing Johnny Kidd's
'Please Don't Touch' at
Exmouth Pavilion

As mentioned in the opening paragraph of this biography, The Graduates, also from Exmouth, 'ran in tandem' with The Royals throughout their heyday, and although rivalry existed between the two outfits, members of both bands were always willing to help out their counterparts.

The Graduates were initially Exeter based and fronted by vocalist Barry Woodward.

A disagreement between certain members of the band led Barry to leave the Exeter outfit and form his own band. He chose to keep the name Graduates, and recruited musicians from the Exmouth area: rhythm guitarist Mike 'Gribbles' Beckett, lead guitarist John Kirton, top local drummer Howard Clarke and bass player Brian England. Gribbles, the nickname by which he is best known even today, was as a child very nervous, and suffering from a hearing disorder which for many years went undetected.

This made lessons terribly difficult for the boy, and he was frequently the butt of cruel jibes from his classmates. This situation was rectified when Mike started to play the guitar. He became a minor celebrity, and suddenly found that he had lots of friends. A customer at his parent's fish and chip shop gave Mike his unusual nickname. The man peered over the top of the counter and said to the youngster, 'You're not tall enough to be a chip, and not wide enough to be a piece of fish, you're more like a gribble.' (He meant those small crunchy bits of cooked batter often called scraps or scrapings).

By the time that Barry Woodward's Mk II Graduates decided to disband, Gribbles had deputised for Royals guitarist Keith Heaton on many occasions, and was the obvious choice as rhythm guitarist with the Collins brothers' new group, The Law.

Together with Terry, Mick and Gribbles, bass player Mike 'Dapper' Down from Okehampton, and local singer Robin Ford, The Law benefited from the combined knowledge of both The Royals and the Graduates, and the 'new sound' brought immediate results.

In December 1966, The Law was contracted by the Argus Entertainment's Agency in Seaton, to play the Star Palast circuit in Germany. Bunky Collins explained to the agent that his kid brother was only fifteen years old and that all the members of the band would need passports. It was agreed that the band would delay the tour until Mick's sixteenth birthday, a matter of a few weeks. Two days before they were due to sail, Gribbles and the boys travelled to the Passport Office in London, collected the paperwork and returned to Exmouth to obtain a doctor's signature as required.

In the early hours of the morning on departure day, the battered Renault van was loaded up and the band left their homes once more, bound for the Passport Office and Germany. The passports were collected, and Gribbles was carefully weaving his way through the traffic in the centre of London when the van suddenly ground to a halt. The vehicle was pushed to the kerbside where it was discovered that one of the drive shafts had sheared off. Telephone calls were hastily made to Albert Collins and Gribble's stepfather and remarkably, within five hours, they had purchased a replacement van, a Commer costing £40 from a garage in Axminster, sorted out the insurance details, and driven to London.

Heading once again for Dover, Gribbles quickly became familiar with the vagaries of the vehicle and, except for the gear stick which seemed to wobble all over the place, the van appeared to be OK. Gribbles recollects that they could actually see the ferry that was to take them across the Channel when the gear stick broke off. Young Mick, who travelled nowhere without his tool kit, did a temporary repair using bits of wire, but the vehicle still had to be pushed the final couple of metres on to the ferry.

On the Continent, the van was found to have another little fault. The windscreen wipers motor packed up and was duly fixed using a length of good old Westcountry binder twine which when tied to the individual wiper arms and fed through the front windows allowed the wipers to be dragged across the screen manually.

Like many other bands from the United Kingdom contracted to play the Star Palast circuit, The Law experienced monetary problems and six weeks after their arrival in Germany, they contacted the Argus agency in Seaton who released them from their contract.

With the exception of a club/pub named Uncle Tony's Salbatribe, owned by an ardent admirer of Adolf Hitler whose picture adorned the walls, the boys loved Germany and the people. They had made many friends in Dortmund, Kiel and Wuppertaal and having elected to find their own bookings, found these allies invaluable. Finding regular work, however, sufficient to feed, clothe and house four persons in a strange country is not the easiest of tasks, and The Law returned to England after only three months, disbanding shortly after that. Mick, Gribbles, and Dapper Down met regularly following the break up of The Law, and were musically reunited in a band called Shotgun Express.

L–R: Terry, 'Gribbles', Mick, Paddy, Dapper Down

The Scorpions Rock Band
formerly The Avengers

Scorpions are usually desert-dwelling insects, generally accepted to be relatives of spiders, mites, ticks and harvestmen. Of the class *Arachnida*, it is thought that there are over 1000 species worldwide. They are characterised by an elongated body, tipped with a venomous stinger.

The East Devon species of scorpion (now extinct) dwelt in Newton Poppleford, on the A3052 between Exeter and Lyme Regis. Of the class of 1960, this particular species featured a left-handed bass player and his guitar-playing brother who were also close friends.

The country and western band that was performing in the Pig and Whistle Bar at Butlins holiday camp, Clacton-on-Sea, so impressed teenage friends Peter Adey and Geoffrey Gigg, that on their return to Newton Poppleford, they decided to form their own group. It transpired that Peter was a natural musician. In just a few weeks, following the purchase of his first guitar, he was able to play several chords and pick out melody lines with ease and was the obvious choice as lead guitarist. Similarly, Geoff Gigg rapidly learned the most frequently used chords and was happy to play rhythm guitar. Local boys George Crabb and John Baker were co-opted as drummer and vocalist respectively, leaving the new group lacking only a bass guitarist, but Pete Adey thought he had the answer.

Brothers Vince and Pete Adey

Returning to his home at 22 School Lane, sometimes referred to as Vicarage Road, Newton Poppleford, Peter asked his younger brother Vince if he fancied playing bass guitar. 'I'll give it a go, but I'll need some cash to buy one,' replied Vince, who sauntered off to 'tap up' Mum and Dad for a bridging loan.

Avengers: (L–R) Vince Adey, John Baker, George Crabb, Pete Adey, Geoff Gigg

Practice makes perfect

Mum and Dad Adey (Bet and Fred) were convinced that this was a Vince-con and not altogether certain that they actually wanted two guitarists in the house, but like many parents before and since, assisted their son in buying his first instrument. A second-hand Burns sonic bass guitar, the only left-handed bass in the shop, further discounted by the kindly Bill Greenhalgh, soon occupied pride of place in Vince's bedroom.   With the minimum of tuition from brother Peter, Vince quickly mastered the basics and proudly took his place in the front line of the group.

The Avengers was the name democratically selected by the band prior to its first full practice at the Royal British Legion Club (Newton Poppleford Branch), a wooden hut near St Luke's Church. Incidentally, the British Legion was the beneficiary of the band's first public performance at the village hall, where The Avengers gave their services free of charge in appreciation of being allowed to use the club for their rehearsals.

Look at me when I'm talking to you!

Rock and roll was the 'in thing', and the five lads just loved it. Equally importantly, so did the teenagers from not only Newton Poppleford, but the surrounding villages as well. Playing both instrumental and vocal numbers, The Avengers amassed a comprehensive play-list and thoroughly enjoyed their first year 'under the spotlight'.

At the beginning of 1962 Pete Adey spotted an item in a local newspaper, announcing that The Avengers were playing at the Mariner's Hall in Beer. 'Can't remember taking that booking' thought a bemused Peter before the penny dropped. Sure enough Peter confirmed at a practice session that day that an inconsiderate group of musicians from Tiverton, already an established outfit, were called The Avengers. *(Sorry lads. Barry Sowden, formerly lead guitarist of The Avengers, Tiverton.)*

Discussions regarding a change of name noted that The Beatles were a very high-profile act, and insects kept cropping up – but termites, spiders and the like simply did not have the same 'ring' to them. Then someone said, 'What about calling us The Scorpions?'

The change of identity appeared to breathe new life into the band, and although, for personal reasons, vocalist John Baker left, his place at the front being taken by local man and cousin to Geoff Gigg, Terry French, the popularity of the band soared.

The Scorpions, or The Scorpion Rock Band as their publicity card incorrectly states, were much in demand. Bet and Fred Adey gave the distinct impression that their telephone would be less busy if their number was changed to Colaton Raleigh 999 rather than 520, but in Peter's absence would regularly accept bookings on the band's behalf.

In addition to the many village hall committees within the East Devon area, all anxious to hire the group for their fund-raising enterprises, The Scorpions were frequently engaged to play in the Somerset area by Frank Huddy, an entertainment agent based in Chard.

Edward Lucas, Exmouth

The Reason Why: Reg Bagwell, far left; Richard Bagwell second right

During 1964, Peter, who for several years had 'dabbled' on the piano at home, decided that he liked the sound obtained by several of the chart-topping bands that featured an organ in their line-up. He bought a Farfisa Compact electronic organ and was later invited to become a member of The Reason Why, a band from Ottery St Mary founded by the Bagwell brothers, Reg and Richard, following the break up of The Cyclones (See *Oh No! It's Local Rock and Roll* – Mid Devon edition, for the Cyclones' biography).

Without lead guitarist Peter, The Scorpions lost momentum and disbanded. Younger brother Vince moved to Exmouth, eventually teaming up with Dave Green's Midnight Blues. It is thought that Geoff Gigg forsook the comparative tranquillity of Newton Poppleford for the altogether faster pace of Bristol. Vocalists John Baker and Terry French, and drummer George Crabb remain residents in East Devon.

The Secrets

In a moment of whimsy, I thought of starting this biography by asking you, the reader, to guess the names of the musicians who formed the band of the title, and when asked to reveal the answer say, 'I can't tell you, it's a secret'.

This would of course be rather silly, but text in this vein did appear in the *South West Scene* magazine, launched in 1964. The fortnightly publication costing 1/- (5p) catered strictly for teenagers, and gave the latest information on local groups, venues, and vocalists. Sadly, only four issues were ever produced.

The Tuxedos at Countess Wear Youth Club

In 1963, following the break-up of both the short-lived Tuxedos and The Vincents and after a brief spell with the Harlequins, guitarist Colin Drake teamed up with childhood friend and vocalist Alan 'Kaiser' Bryant. Together with rhythm guitarist Dave Evans, the diminutive, technically brilliant former Starfire's bass guitarist Brian Nott and a superb drummer called Tommy Gibson, they launched The Secrets on to the unsuspecting dance-going public of Exeter.

All with several years of experience under their belts, the five musicians needed very little rehearsal to display an aura of confidence to their audience.

On the rare occasions when it was deemed necessary to meet and *perhaps* practise a new number, the five young men would meet at Marcini's Dance Studio, run by Tommy's mother Marsena from her large house in Colleton Crescent, Exeter, near the Hourglass public house, set up the equipment in the huge cellar, run quickly through the song, and settle down for a chat and a coffee.

The regular Saturday-morning visit to Bill Greenhalgh's shop took care of any advertising that the band felt was necessary to inform the public of its existence. Most musicians will be aware that there is no better advertisement for a band's capabilities than by word of mouth. Working bands will readily pass the news of a new outfit's formation to club secretaries, agents and dance promoters, because musicians invariably try to help one another – and there was no better place to meet other musicians than at Bill's on a Saturday.

Suffice to say that The Secrets became established on the local scene quite quickly. Initially, the bookings were confined to village halls, Dolton and Morchard Bishop being just two of many. As the band's reputation grew, and demand soared, gigs at the Athena Club and the Civic Hall in Exeter followed.

Tony Harper

Torquay agent Lionel Digby, ever on the lookout for fresh talent, heard the boys at America Hall in Pinhoe. Double-billed with Gary Kane and the Tornadoes, The Secrets acquitted themselves exceptionally well. Lionel liked what he had heard and signed the boys to his agency soon after. As it happened, Tony Harper, stage name Tony London, The Tornadoes' drummer, would later join The Secrets, replacing Tommy Gibson who was to turn professional with Chico Arnez and his Latin American Dance Orchestra.

A stroke of genius from band leader Colin Drake brought vocalist Tony Osborne into the band. The Secrets became 'special' virtually overnight, the dual voices of 'Kaiser' and 'Ozzie' augmented by the backing vocals of rhythm guitarist Dave Evans, enabling the band to perform numbers with complex harmonies. Tony adopted the stage name Barry B. Silent, and Alan responded by announcing that he would in future perform under the name Chris Younge.

By kind permission of Lionel Digby, who knew a good band when he saw one, The Secrets featuring Barry B. Silent and Chris Younge, became frequent visitors to Torbay, appearing regularly at both the '400' Club and the Town Hall in Torquay.

It was at the latter that Tony Osborne developed a new stage act, Exeter's answer to the 'Rocky Horror Show'. Booked as the support act to Screaming Lord Such and the Savages, The Secrets opened the proceedings, warming the crowd for the professional artistes, who had been booked to provide a one-and-a-half-hour cabaret spot midway through the evening's entertainment. Having completed their first set, The Secrets gave way to The Savages who took the stage looking drawn, apprehensive, and anything but savage – unlike the fee-paying, ticket-holding audience who were

The Secrets at Countess Wear Youth Club: (L–R) Dave, Brian, Tony, Colin; front Tony Osborne (Barry B. Silent), Alan Bryant (Chris Younge)

impatiently awaiting the arrival of Screaming Lord Such … as were The Savages. An excellent band, The Savages provided real value for money, but this appeared to be of little consolation to the natives of Torbay, who were becoming extremely hostile.

Lionel Digby, by this time a worried man, sought out Tony Osborne and informed him that The Secrets would have to go back on and do some sort of 'horror act'. Luckily, Dave 'Screaming Lord' Such arrived in the nick of time, wowed the crowd, and spared the blushes of both The Savages and The Secrets. The events of the evening had, however, given Tony Osborne food for thought.

With considerable pre-planning and a gallon of greasepaint, Tony gradually developed his own 'horror show'. The act was 'premiered' at a rather swish hotel in Paignton, much to the consternation of the management. Highlights of the act included 'strangling' bass player Brian Nott, and hitting drummer Tony Harper on the head with his own floor-standing tom-tom. The act was hugely popular with audiences everywhere, although things did occasionally go awry.

Memorable mishaps included the near asphyxiation of a bass player by an over-enthusiastic singer, the batter-head (skin) of a floor-standing tom-tom breaking over an astonished and unhappy drummer's head, and a co-singer with severe bruising to the lumbar area. Alan's injuries resulted from Tony lifting him bodily, cackling maniacally all the while, his foot becoming entangled with a microphone lead and both men and a PA amplifier crashing to the floor, Tony having much the softer landing by falling on top of Alan. Apparently, a concerned Dave Evans had leapt forward and was greatly relieved to find that the amplifier was undamaged.

With the possible exception of Brian Nott (he of the regularly abused epiglottis), the act never failed to attract and amuse the dance-goers of

Devon. The Starline connection enabled their counterparts in Cornwall to be similarly entertained. When Brian Roberts, the proprietor of Starline Entertainments was requested to send The Secrets to both Tabbs, and the Flamingo Club in Redruth, he hastily contacted Colin Drake and signed the band to his agency.

Now contracted to LMD *and* Starline Entertainments the group became busier than ever, and while they strove to play locally whenever possible, they enjoyed the odd jaunt over the border. The Cornish teenagers always gave The Secrets, who were invariably described as a touring band, a warm welcome, and it was a pleasant drive down the old A30 to Redruth. Additionally, it was a well-paid job. But the main reason for their unmitigated joy upon receipt of yet another Tabbs booking was a small café immediately opposite the club, which according to singer Alan Bryant, served up the best sausage and chips he had ever tasted.

There were, of course, times when the proprietors 'shut up shop' early, closing the front door at midnight, defiantly refusing to appease the pangs of hunger raging in the stomachs of five ravenous musicians, stating that he had been open since eleven o'clock that morning and was 'dog-tired'. This would call for plan 'B'. The return journey to Exeter would be timed to coincide with the opening of a little baker's shop in Alphington Road. The Secrets had their timing off to a 'T', generally arriving on, or approaching 'Mr Bun's' doorstep at exactly 5am. Drummer Tony Harper, wearing his trademark bowler hat, would be despatched to acquire freshly baked bread rolls, pasties or pies, for him and the boys. Quirkily, and for reasons unknown but always suspected, Tony's purchase was always carried back to the van hidden under his hat!

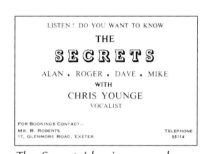

The Secrets' business card

In the summer of 1964, The Secrets experienced a noticeable drop in the amount of bookings received from the two agencies to which they were contracted. Colin Drake contacted both Brian Roberts and Lionel Digby, and was informed that it was becoming ever more difficult to find quality engagements for a five-piece outfit. It appeared that an increasing number of club secretaries, owners of hotels and holiday camps and even Young Farmers' clubs, were restricted by budget, and required three or four-piece bands only. Brian stressed that he was striving constantly to keep all his acts regularly employed, and that when a suitable booking presented itself he would be on the telephone immediately. Lionel practically reiterated Brian's words, but added that an abundance of work existed for a four-piece.

Colin relayed the news to Alan, Tony, Dave, and Tony Harper. The discussion was curtailed by Alan Bryant's announcement that he would leave the band. He was confident that he could join another group, and hoped that his departure would ensure that the remaining members of The Secrets would continue to be at the top of the agent's availability list. He was proved right on both counts. Alan became a member of the highly rated Bluesounds, and The Secrets continued to enjoy local success during the months that lay ahead.

Serendipity

There are two reasons why Serendipity should not really feature here. Firstly, the band was not formed until the mid-1970s which barely meets the chronological criteria of this book. Secondly, the band was not in essence a rock and roll outfit, although this musical genre generally featured in its stunning repertoire. There are many more reasons why the band's biography has been included. Now read on.

Serendipity began life in the Exmouth area as a vocal harmony cabaret act consisting of husband-and-wife-team David and Marilyn Vane, and Michael Glancy, known as Mick. The trio had enjoyed a modicum of success locally, and built a loyal and appreciative fan-base. The instrumental accompaniment to the three voices was provided by David, who skilfully combined hands and feet by operating a set of bass pedals whilst playing guitar, and guitarist Mick, who found a single fretboard plenty to be getting on with.

The proprietor of a music centre in Exmouth trading under his own name, David had for many years harboured the desire to lead a bigger band. In January 1976, having consulted with Marilyn and Mick, he began to both rearrange and augment the trio. Mick Glancy agreed to become the new band's bass player, and the original complement was doubled at a stroke with the addition of Ian Briggs, Alan Haydon, and Dave Smale.

Tenor- and alto-saxophonist Ian Briggs also excelled on the harmonica, upon which pocket-sized piece of kit he would later become national champion in the blues category.

Experienced tenor- and soprano-saxophonist Alan Haydon had done his apprenticeship with outfits like Son-Set, Dance Scene, and The River Set; he was a first-class reader of music, and also possessed the capability to busk with the best.

L–R: Alan Haydon, Ian Briggs, Dave Huxham

Much-travelled Dave Smale was quite simply a superb drummer, metronome-like timing and attention to detail making him a class act. Rehearsals were fun, and enjoyed by all, the 'all-raced all rallied' line-up able to encompass a wide range of music. The vocals were shared by band leader Dave, Marilyn and Mick, and the diary filled at almost the same rate as the play-list.

Marilyn left the band in June 76, and husband David immediately drafted in a replacement. Granted, the replacement wasn't as attractive as Marilyn, neither could he sing like her, but Dave Huxham was a fine multi-instrumentalist, adept on trumpet, flugelhorn and keyboard.

There were now three members of Serendipity called Dave. This led to Dave Smale becoming 'Big Dave, and Dave Huxham becoming 'Diddy Dave, or just 'Diddy'. After each rehearsal, 'Boss Dave' ensured that each member of the band was completely aware of all relevant matters appertaining to the outfit, and welcomed their ideas and comments, which prompted Alan Haydon to refer to his band leader as 'Democratic Dave'.

David, as opposed to Big or Diddy, persuaded the other members of the band to invest in a lighting-rig and a more powerful PA system. Stage attire was updated and improved, the band now wearing ivory-coloured three-piece suits, and although David was himself a fine musical arranger, professionally scored sheet music was regularly bought.

Investments were carefully controlled, and the band was listed as a registered company, each of the current members becoming a director. Serendipity became the Serendipity Showband and began to receive bookings from all over the West of England, most of which were accepted and fulfilled. Concerned that the big sound produced by the various instruments would appear 'garbled' through the amplification presently being used by the band, Dave proposed that a mixing-desk be purchased. This, he suggested, would allow a dedicated channel for each instrument, which could be individually controlled, thereby achieving the correct balance and tonal quality.

The equipment was duly acquired and became an integral part of David Vane's continual quest for perfection in sound. The desk was operated by Richard 'Dick' Childs, a man with a 'good ear'. Dick stayed with the Showband for six months or so before being replaced by Martin Fowler. The latter was the consummate roadie, able to both erect and dismantle the desk, lighting gantry and all amplification in additional to controlling sound and lighting. Also responsible for the recruitment of extra road crew when required, Martin remained with the band throughout.

Serendipity Limited now required a truck to convey the mountain of equipment, and a minibus for the musicians. Both items were bought, and as the band became increasingly more professional in sound and attitude, the boys rarely set up their own gear, preferring to entrust the job to Martin who would go on ahead with the truck, leaving the boys in the band to follow in the minibus, normally arriving at the venue in time for a sound check.

In March 1977, the Serendipity Showband successfully auditioned to become the resident act at the Top Rank Suite in Plymouth, appearing on Tuesday, Wednesday, and Thursday nights. The trio of midweek bookings allowed the band to retain their own weekend work, thus keeping in touch with their audiences in Exeter and East Devon.

A recurring problem for outfits 'in residency' is the need to constantly rehearse and update the library, mainly to keep boredom at bay and the repertoire fresh. Serendipity developed nine 45-minute sets, which could be

Serendipity fronted by Kim Martin

mixed and matched at will. In a manner reminiscent of the routines that The Ginger Walker Band was currently belting out on the North Devon circuit, they would perform any set non-stop. The band's stage presentation was further improved by varying the dress code for each routine and total abstinence from smoking or drinking whilst on stage.

These express routines were always followed by a complete change in both mood and tempo. After one particular rock and roll thrash, Mick informed the near-exhausted audience that he was going to sing his version of The Beatles' haunting and melodic 'Long and Winding Road'. Given a single note by 'Diddy Dave', Mick pitched into the opening bars of the song.

Keyboard player Alan Lisk

No one knows quite how the well-rehearsed and normally efficient Diddy came to hit the wrong note, but the words 'winding road' had hardly left Mick's lips when the entire might of Serendipity entered the fray right on cue, but playing in a completely different key from the one in which Mick had started the number. He was not a happy bunny. Thankfully, such occurrences were rare.

In June of 1977, the management suggested, to the point of insisting, that the Showband employ what they pseudo-trendily termed a 'chick vocalist'. Auditions were held and from the many hopefuls, Kim Martin was chosen. During her sparse leisure time, now further reduced, Kim was an avid tox-opholite (she enjoyed archery). Near national standard, she had developed the muscles in her arms to proportions that were the envy of many a young man, and can only be described as spectacular.

Marilyn and Chrissie

One month later, band leader Dave decided to increase the overall sound still further and added piano and synthesiser player Alan Lisk to the 'payroll'. Diddy Dave Huxham happily surrendered his keyboard duties, to concentrate solely on his trumpet and flugelhorn sounds, and Serendipity was now an eight-piece.

The breakneck pace of the five-nights-a-week schedule began to take its toll

The Serendipity Showband at the Top Rank Suite, Plymouth.

at the end of the summer, drummer Dave Smale deciding that the gruelling pace was just too much. From the incredible Clarke family of drummers, Stuart replaced Dave in September 77. Six months later, Kim Martin had to admit that Dave Smale had been right. The Top Rank management again decreed that a 'chick' singer was a must. Democratic Dave wanted his wife Marilyn to return, but the rest of the boys thought that auditions should be held. The auditions produced a number of probables, but two girls stood out from the rest: Marilyn Vane, who demonstrated that she had lost none of her vivacity, and fully justified her husband's faith in her, and a startlingly attractive girl called Christine Wiblin who worked under the stage name of Chrissie Lee.

The boys in the band could not reach a decision – both girls were out-standing. Dave Vane, given that he was obviously biased (and possibly thinking about the domestic repercussions), abstained from voting. Eventually, and after hours of discussion, deliberation, and analysis, it was agreed that both girls would be taken on. Serendipity was now a nine-piece and, short of adding strings and a woodwind section, David Vane had realised his ambition to lead a big band.

Initially played as a joke, 'The Muppet Show Theme' became the Showband's trademark opening and closing number. Chrissie Lee developed a sensational version of the Kiki Dee number 'I've Got the Music in Me' which linked neatly with the Muppet theme, and the audience appeared to enjoy the closing sequence equally as much, if not more, as any part of the evening's programme.

After two full years at the Top Rank Suite, the members of Serendipity began to feel the pressure, largely caused by burning the candle at both ends. There were also administrative difficulties. Serendipity were registered for VAT and those members who had full-time jobs outside of the band and were not self-employed, were required to pay two National Insurance contributions.

David Vane was adamant that Serendipity should turn professional at the earliest possible moment, and wife Marilyn was in full agreement. The others, however, were against the idea, which drove a wedge into the heart of the band. David and Marilyn formed a new outfit, and retained the contract to play at the Top Rank.

Free of bureaucratic restrictions, the boys – not forgetting Chrissie Lee – discontinued their VAT registration. Mike 'Gribbles' Beckett, former rhythm guitarist with The Graduates and The Law, was recruited as a replacement for David Vane, and the band continued to perform as Serendipity right across the West Country, but at weekends only. The decrease in workload provided the fillip that Chrissie and the boys needed, and they began to enjoy themselves once again.

But Serendipity's world fell apart after just one year following the split with David and Marilyn Vane. Chrissie Lee was offered a job as a courier with travel firm Cosmos, and decided to accept. Keyboards wizard Alan Lisk moved out of the area to join a professional dance company in London, and Ian Briggs and Mick Glancy decided to form a blues band. Replacing half a band quickly was an impossible task, and the remaining members went their separate ways. Alan teamed up yet again with Pete Evans in his band Nice 'n' Easy, and Stuart, Gribbles, and 'Diddy' joined drummer Steve Orgée in forming a soul band.

Serendipity's last public appearance was on 27 March 1980 at HMS *Drake* in Plymouth when they took second billing to Freddie and the Dreamers.

Admission ticket to Samantha's, Exmouth

Serendipity with Mike 'Gribbles' Beckett

The Son-Set and Dance Scene

Formerly the bass guitarist with Gary Kane's Tornadoes, Alan Maggs founded the Son-Set in the autumn of 1966 with well-known and extremely proficient local guitarist John West. Musically speaking, the line-up was completed by drummer Mike Ewings whose father Bob managed the trio during the early days.

Within six months of its inception the trio had become a quintet by the addition of Alan Haydon and Roger Betts. Guitarist Alan Haydon, a teacher at Elmore Junior School, Tiverton, was equally at home playing the saxophone, and had previously played the banjo with the East Side Jazzmen. Organist Roger Betts, who had recently moved into the area from Coventry, was a teacher at Heathcoat Junior School in Tiverton, and was lodging with Alan and Maureen Haydon at their cottage in the hamlet of Bolham.

The five-piece took to the road in January 1967, their first gig being at the popular Grenville Club on the A38 at the foot of Haldon Hill, south of Exeter. Their easy style and competent performance, which belied the fact that the outfit had been playing together for only a short time, won them many friends and led to offers of work throughout the county in village, town, and city halls, hotels, sports clubs, colleges and military establishments.

Somewhat less popular with the band were the functions held at local rugby clubs, the over-enthusiastic members of which would habitually celebrate winning and commiserate a loss in much the same fashion, by imbibing gallons of beer. The traditional 'boat-race' (if you don't know, enquire at your local rugby club) inevitably resulted in the dance floor becoming awash with ale by the end of the evening.

The Son-Set 'flying high' at Exeter Airport in 1967

At the home of Exmouth 'Cockles', following a particularly raucous but enjoyable and trouble-free evening, Son-Set were packing up when Alan Haydon spotted a pile of sodden music on the floor. Gingerly picking up the music between thumb and index finger Alan said to organist Roger Betts, 'Hey Rog, look at the state of your dots (music)!' Glancing at the music, Roger replied, 'That's OK, It's not a problem.'

Amazed, Alan asked, 'Why ever not?'
Grinning, Roger said, 'Because it's not my music, it's yours.'

In June of the same year, Son-Set embarked on a series of mid-week appearances at the Dawlish Sands Holiday Camp, and four weeks later were offered a summer season at a hotel also in Dawlish, the Grand. The additional work caused immediate problems. Band leader Alan Maggs wanted to take up the Grand option, as did Alan Haydon and Roger Betts, whilst John and Mike Ewings were happy to continue at Dawlish Sands. An impasse was reached and Alan Maggs recruited guitarist Mike Emery and drummer Dave Denning, the brother of former Nightlights, Starfires, and Guild drummer Terry, to replace John and Mike. Dave's day job meant that he was not always available mid-week and, among several others, ex-Codiak Pete Evans and young Janet Pring frequently sat in.

Janet was the drummer who had the most impact visually. The sister of Pete Evans' trumpet-playing girlfriend Pauline, she was depping with Son-Set at a function held at Seale Hayne College. On arriving at Seale Hayne, the band was greeted by the college principal, who presumed that Janet was the girlfriend of one of the group and, apart from a cursory nod and a curt good evening, did not bring her into the conversation. He was later taken aback to see the young lady adeptly setting up a drum-kit and this time incorrectly assumed that she was the drummer's girlfriend. He did, however, notice that Janet was wearing slacks. Striding purposefully to the stage he sternly informed her that he did not allow girls to wear trousers in college. Unfazed by this male chauvinism, Janet momentarily toyed with the idea of playing in her underwear, then strolled to the van, retrieved the skirt that she had worn while travelling to the college, popped into the ladies' powder room to change, and nonchalantly drummed up a storm throughout the evening.

The Grand Hotel in which Son-Set were placed on four evenings of each week scarcely lived up to its name. The menu seemed to consist of chicken and chips in the basket and, as the musicians quickly discovered, if you remained standing for too long in certain sections of the lounge bar, you would stick to the carpet!

Occasionally, the hotel management complained about the volume of the music, and Alan Maggs never failed to issue the instruction to turn everything down. On one particular evening Alan was convinced that his band were playing at a sensible, easy-listening volume and that the overall balance was right. When the manager insisted that the volume was too loud, Alan snapped!

Turning his bass amplifier off, he repeated the action with the PA system then ordered Mike Emery and Roger Betts to turn their amplifiers off also. Geoff Bulley who had solved the 'different drummer every night crisis' by agreeing to join the band on a permanent basis was instructed to play with his hands, and Alan Haydon and his saxophone were banished to the gentlemen's lavatory adjacent to the stage.

To the amusement of the assembled audience, none of whom had complained about the volume, the band leader counted in the band rather louder than was usual for the benefit of the exiled Alan Haydon, and Son-Set played their first-ever song 'unplugged'. Perhaps not surprisingly, the manager favoured neither the petulant and sarcastically tinged example of the band's acoustic prowess, or the barely audible volume at which it was presented, and a compromise was reached during the next interval.

Although this was the age of 'flower-power', peace and love, with the latest waxings from artists like Scott McKenzie and the Flower Pot Men a permanent fixture on every jukebox, the members of Son-Set felt that a change was in the offing, and that soul music was about to break on to the scene. With this in mind, Roger, Alan Haydon, Mike Emery, and drummer Geoff Bulley began rehearsing with old friend, formerly a drummer and now a bass player, Pete Evans and his girlfriend Pauline Pring. The practice sessions, usually held in the upstairs foyer of the Odeon cinema in Exeter, quickly paid dividends.

In November 1967, at a time when Procol Harum were topping the UK charts with the classic 'Whiter Shade of Pale', Alan Maggs decided that it was the right moment to move on. A thoughtful and dedicated group man, Alan gave the band adequate notice of his intentions. A major shake-up saw Chris Abrahams installed as the new front man, Mike Aldridge was drafted into the rhythm section on bass guitar, and Alan Haydon donned the mantle of band leader. With this line-up the band went from strength to strength, attracting bookings of an even higher quality throughout 1968.

A devotee of soul music, Chris Abrahams adopted the stage-name of Cleveland Jones. A total extrovert, he dressed as wildly as he performed, his stage dress completed with an amazing pair of luminous, brightly spotted boots. His personal repertoire of soul music appeared to be boundless and he was blessed with a powerful voice. The owner of possibly the first pair of Vox column speakers to be seen in the Exeter and East Devon District, Chris was extremely proud of them.

The advertising jingle alleging that 'Things go better with Coca-Cola' was firmly disproved when some was accidentally spilt on to Chris Abrahams' amplifier; the unit hissed and 'died', the valves rendered useless. Showing foresight and professionalism, Chris reached into his gig bag, produced a set of replacement valves, fitted them to the amplifier and, after a short break in proceedings, continued as though the incident had not occurred.

New Year's Eve 1967 found Son-Set at the Flamingo Club in Redruth, Cornwall. Trumpet player Pauline Pring had been added to the line-up to boost the sound for the special occasion. Taking a well-deserved break, Pauline was gently tickling the ivories on the in-house piano at the side of the stage, and as usual was being chatted up by a drunk claiming to have played the cornet, trumpet or bugle with a local brass band, Boys' Brigade, or school orchestra.

'Do you play by ear?' he slurred. Pauline's normal good humour deserted her. 'No, I play with me bum, she replied, watch!' Turning her back on the piano, Pauline slid up and down the keys on her bottom. Unfortunately, the Cornishman had the last laugh. Pauline's silk dress ripped from side to side. Like a trouper, she completed the gig but ensured that she faced the audience throughout.

The acquisition of group transport in the shape of a BMC J2 van seemed to make perfect economic sense, one vehicle being used to convey both musicians and equipment instead of four cars as had previously been the case. The band-wagon, acquired from Samuel Beeston's Music Shop in Bampton Street, Tiverton, had been used to deliver pianos, and the floor had been reinforced with a half-inch-thick (12mm) steel plate. The 'armour-plated' floor, undoubtedly the vehicle's sole redeeming feature, was the only metallic part unaffected by rust.

Cursed with a column gear change, the van's lever broke off in driver Chris Abraham's hand as he engaged second gear whilst returning from a gig one evening. The van was nursed back to Exeter in second gear, a distance of some 20 miles.

Despite its odd mechanical foible, the boys loved the little vehicle, not least because of the 'van-test'. The J2 was a forward-control vehicle, which meant that the driver and front passenger were seated immediately above the front wheels and separated by the raised engine cover. Additional bench seating had been fitted behind a bulkhead to the rear of the driver's compartment, access to which, when the van was laden with gear, was by climbing over the engine cover and through the bulkhead,(12mm), a simple matter for anyone wearing trousers, but not as easy for any girl travelling with the band wearing a skirt.

Both the driver (usually Chris Abrahams), passenger and the remaining members of the band who were also to sit in the rear, would chivalrously jump out, assist the lady into the van, and observe her futile struggle to protect her modesty through the windscreen. Some giggling girls had to make several attempts!

During the two years that Son-Set was on the local scene, the boys acted as support band for many famous outfits: Simon Dupree and the Big Sound, John Mayall's Bluesbreakers, and The Searchers, to name but three. On the flip side of this coin, Son-Set were often supported by a band from Torquay called The Empty Vessels who later became Wishbone Ash.

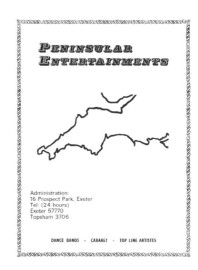

Front cover of Peninsular Entertainment brochure

In mid-September 1968, Roger Betts accepted an invitation to work with The Maurice Price Band at Tiffany's in Exeter. The experience proved to be less enjoyable than anticipated, and he returned to Son-Set just a few weeks later. Geoff Bulley also felt that it was time for a change, having been offered the chance to team up with his childhood friends Ray Pope and the author of this book, in a band that was to enjoy much success, Nashville Skyline. Like Alan Maggs before him, Geoff awaited his replacement Pete Greenham prior to leaving the band.

Pressure of work forced bass player Mike Aldridge to call it a day at the end of 1968. Mike Emery agreed to forsake his guitar to become the bass player as a temporary measure, but in the event Mike's dexterity seemed to suit all concerned, and the move became permanent. When Mike Emery finally left Son-Set, John Haydon, the brother of band leader Alan, supplanted him. John remained with the band until the very end.

In January 1969, drummer Pete Greenham and vocalist Chris Abrahams decided that they too would call it a day. Son-Set played its last gig at Killerton House, which at that time was a hall of residence for St Luke's College. It was a great night!

The dissolution of Son-Set coincided with that of an Exeter-based outfit, Future Impressions. Roger Betts and Alan Haydon late of Son-Set, and Peter and Pauline Evans (née Pring) of Future Impressions were old friends and had played together many times. It was providence that both bands had broken up virtually simultaneously, and a new band appeared to be 'just around the corner'.

Dance Scene was the name chosen for the amalgam and comprised: leader and bass guitarist Pete Evans with his wife Pauline on trumpet, organist Roger Betts, Alan Haydon playing tenor and soprano saxophones and guitar, drummer Roger Youldon, and vocalist Terry Carnell. The latter possessed neither a PA system, nor the wherewithal to buy one; what he did have was a microphone, a very good voice and tons of charisma.

Dance Scene featuring Terry Carnell and Phil Snell

'Just pulling your leg'

The solution to the PA problem lay in a small black box, which trisected the signal from Terry's microphone. The three signals were then routed to a spare channel in each of the guitar, keyboard, and bass amplifiers. The system worked well, and it gave Terry time to accumulate the necessary funds required to obtain a purpose-built system, breathing space for which he was very grateful, for a very long time! A brilliant front man, Terry was at his best when talking from a stage, and especially to the female section of the audience.

Dance Scene rehearsed regularly and by the end of 1970 was much in demand, especially for parties. One of Terry's favourite party pieces was to inform the audience that he was going to sing a very popular song which featured the words 'Leap up and down and wave your knickers in the air', and that a spot prize would be given to the first lady brave enough to 'get 'em off.'

Knickers!

Having issued this invitation to a lively audience at the Green Headlands Hotel (now the Parkway Hotel) at Sampford Peverell to the north of Tiverton, Terry momentarily turned away from the audience to adjust the volume on his microphone. A split second later he turned round to find a young woman proudly holding proof that she had accepted his challenge.

Terry spluttered and refused to believe that she had in fact 'got 'em off', and insisted that she had taken them from her handbag, whereupon she lifted her skirt to waist level and said, 'Oh no I bloody well didn't!'

The other members of the band had seen her actually remove the garment, and fell about laughing, unable to play for several minutes. Meanwhile, Terry instigated a whip-round to buy ten cigarettes from the bar as a spot prize for

Dance Scene with, standing centre stage, bass player Tony Charman

the adventurous young woman, who by this time appeared to have taken on celebrity status.

After a year or so together, outside pressures began to take their toll. Pressures of work, and the need for a change generally, caused the band to amicably split-up. After only four months Dance Scene was reincarnated. In September of 1972, having enjoyed the respite period but now bored senseless, Roger Betts decided to buy a set of bass pedals for his keyboard,

The River Set at the Fisherman's Cot, Bickleigh

and also to acquire a bass guitar. With Alan Haydon doubling on saxes and guitar, it was necessary only to re-recruit Terry Carnell and find a drummer, for Dance Scene Mk II to work adequately as a four-piece.

Drummer Alan Winmill had recently moved to Exeter having bought the record shop next door to Bill Greenhalgh's Music Mart on Fore Street Hill, and was snapped up by Dance Scene in short order. Alan drummed with the band for about six months before he succumbed, like many musicians before him, to the tension caused by continual late nights and early-bird starts and he left the 'Scene', to be replaced by Steve Orgée.

In September 1973, just twelve months after the rebirth of the band, Roger Betts was finding it increasingly difficult to work his day job in with his hobby. Purely as a stopgap, a deputy was found in Brian Ley, but Brian too had work commitments and, although happy to occasionally stand in for Roger, would not accept the job full-time. Roger reluctantly parted company with the band in October.

Alan added two musicians in an attempt to counteract the missing organ sound, Phil Snell – much travelled and experienced saxophonist – and bass guitarist Tony 'Tone the Coat' Charman. Alan gave up playing the saxophone to concentrate on his guitar, but the line-up changed once again when Phil Snell left. Chris Lane was brought in on guitar, which allowed Alan to return to juggling saxophones and guitar.

Dance Scene was becoming more pop orientated with Chris, Tony and Steve wanting to play in a louder, more aggressive style. Many of the venues, cultivated over the years by both Dance Scene, and Son-Set before them, did not require music of this type and objected strongly to the increase in volume, some agents, club, and hotel owners putting their thoughts on the subject on to paper.

'**BOBSHERUNKLE**'
FOR BOOKING PROCEDURE CONTACT :
Johnny Ramone
Entertainments Consultants
(OVER 20 YEARS IN ENTERTAINMENT)
140 THE WALDRONS,   EMPLOYMENT AGENCIES LICENCE 8W172   TELEPHONE
TIVERTON, DEVON, EX16 5EH   TIVERTON 4185 (DAY & NIGHT)

Undeterred, the three musicians found new venues in which to play, and for a while Alan soldiered on, although he regularly expressed his opinion regarding the 'new-wave' material. Alan finally accepted that the band was heading in a direction that was definitely not to his liking, gave notice of his intention to quit, and left in August 1974, subsequently joining the resident band at the Fisherman's Cot Hotel, The River Set.

Bobsheruncle:
(L–R) Graham Isaac, Steve
Orgée, Tony Charman

The three remaining members of Dance Scene changed their name to Oasis (No dear, not *that* Oasis). Graham Isaac replaced Chris Lane shortly after Alan's departure, and the band became Bobsheruncle.

The Velvet Touch and Pride

If his father had not been a civil servant and as such relocated on a fairly regular basis, Neil Govier might not have been mentioned within the pages of this particular book. However, his name would certainly have appeared in a forthcoming work entitled, *Oh No! It's Local Rock and Roll …but I like it!* – the North Devon volume.

Dick Darlison

Neil was born in Braunton, North Devon, in March 1950, and moved to Exeter just before his tenth birthday where he attended the Mount Radford Independent School. He became a member of the school choir and subsequently joined the voluntary choir of Exeter Cathedral. When school friend Tony Lethbridge, now a well-known local author and manager of Exeter Falcons Speedway Team, left the choir Neil became the lead soloist. Singing with the choirs provided him with an understanding of vocal harmonies and arrangements that would prove invaluable in later life.

The onset of puberty – that terrible time in a boy soprano's life when he realises that he sounds more like Arthur Mullard than Aled Jones – saw Neil leave the choir, and The Beatles upstaged Bach as he started to take a real interest in the pop music being played on the radio.

His first guitar, purchased by his mother as a fourteenth birthday present and totally against the wishes of his father, was a rather battered, second-hand acoustic but young Neil absolutely loved the instrument.

Maggie Reeday, later known as Simone

The son of a piano-playing father, and brother to Richard 'Dick' Darlison, an established musician and member of an Exeter band called The Siroccos, Robert 'Bob' Darlison lived in the same cul-de-sac as Neil, and the two became great friends. Bob's acquisition of a guitar led to the two youngsters spending every available minute in each other's company, learning to play chords and picking out the occasional solo. Neil and Bob were helped tremendously by watching and listening to Richard. His insistence on the need for controlled and thoughtful playing made a lasting impression, and Neil maintains to this day that Dick was one of the best all-round musicians that Exeter ever produced.

By 1964 both Neil and Bob had become reasonably proficient. Bob joined a 'hobby band' from Exeter, and Neil was invited to become a member of an outfit revelling in the name Kayos. Chaos or Kayos, the name adequately described the group. Neil, now the proud owner of both electric guitar and amplifier joined bass player Ray Mallett, later to become a speedway rider with the Exeter Falcons, and drummer Peter 'Mac' McCarthy, along with fellow newcomer, rhythm guitarist Patrick 'Paddy' Young. The boys rehearsed hard and were soon playing in local youth clubs and village halls. The addition of young and attractive Margaret 'Maggie' Reeday, a singer, whose ability was matched only by her enthusiasm, brought a semblance of order to the aptly named Kayos during the relatively short life of the band. Some years later, under the stage name Simone, Maggie's fine voice and professional approach were to achieve national status by winning the ITV talent show 'New Faces'.

Kayos had all but sorted its self out musically. The outfit's biggest problem was the group van, yet another old Bedford with an apparent mind of its own. The vehicle would fire only when it felt inclined and invariably required a bump-start. Fitted with sliding doors on both driver and passenger sides, the latter would detach itself from the runners and fall off after only a couple of miles, whereupon the boys would disembark, rehang the door and continue on their way, nervously awaiting the next blast of cold air which meant that the door once again was lying in the road. There were constant arguments as to who would sit in the centre of the front seat closest to the heater. The 'baby' of the band, Neil was always consigned to the back of the van with the equipment, and Maggie usually won the battle to sit in the front.

Following a booking at South Zeal Village Hall, near Okehampton, in sub-zero temperatures, the van steadfastly refused to start. One of the boys suggested that the van be bump-started down a slight gradient. As turning round was impossible in the narrow country lane, the exercise was carried out with the van in reverse gear. The axle emitted a violent groan, and the vehicle was going absolutely nowhere under its own propulsion. Maggie, Neil, Ray, Mac, and Paddy were stranded, miles from nowhere, with half a packet of cigarettes, tired, hungry, thirsty, freezing cold and generally 'brassed off'.

Local dance promoter Nigel Derby, by whom the band had been booked and who was thankfully still at the dance hall, towed the van together with its unhappy occupants to a car park alongside the A30 where they remained

L–R: Dave Denning, Neil Govier, Ian Whiteway, Patrick Young, Paul Walters, 1970

until their collection later that morning. Neil recollects that the cigarettes were lit one at a time and passed from person to person, and that by the time one reached him, it was almost too hot and too small to grasp.

Neil became acquainted with many budding musicians in these early days. When Kayos folded, old friend Paddy Young who now played keyboards, informed Neil that his band, as yet unnamed, would soon need a rhythm guitarist. Neil attended the next rehearsal, met lead guitarist Paul Walters, bass guitarist Mick Goldsworthy, guitarist André Mac who was happy to play bass or rhythm, and a drummer called Chris, and joined the group.

Chris and André left the group after just a few months having taken the decision to start their own band. They were joined by the ex-keyboard player of John Gregory's Spartans, and drummer Dave Denning, the younger brother of Terry, certainly one of Exeter's best drummers, in forming The Best Remain. The complement of the band that was to shortly become The Velvet Touch was restored to full strength when John Walkie replaced Chris on drums, and vocalist Neil Dennis from Countess Wear in Exeter was recruited as the group's front man.

All teenagers, 'Big Neil' Dennis, 'Little Neil' Govier, John, Paul, Paddy and Mick were guided and managed by Ken Walters, father of lead guitarist Paul. Ken also acted as driver for the band for several months, and provided a rehearsal room within his barber's shop in Princesshay, Exeter. Rehearsals were held on Wednesday evenings, a fact that did not go unnoticed by the occupants of the adjoining premises, which prompted an article in that well-respected local newspaper the *Express and Echo*.

The first public appearances by The Velvet Touch took them to the Devon Arms Inn at Kenton, for which the band was paid £7, and the Cat and Fiddle at Clyst St Mary, where they received £8.50 for their services. Playing mostly chart hits with a smattering of rock and roll – occasionally these amounted to the same thing – the Velvet Touch were a happy-go-lucky group, a fact not lost on a strangely likeable policeman who had pulled the boys over for speeding.

The old Leyland Atlas van had been regularly 'touched-up' with differing shades of whatever colour paint was available. On the Saturday afternoon in question, the policeman, having got the undivided attention of driver Neil Dennis, asked, 'What colour d'you call this then?' 'It's psychedelic,' replied Neil. 'Can't spell that,' said the laughing policeman, 'Off you go, oh and by the way, keep your flamin' speed down!'

Mick Goldsworthy was a character and no mistake. Rather than carry his weighty bass speaker cabinets down any flight of stairs that happened to access the function room at some venues, especially after carrying them upstairs in the first instance, he would simply tote them to the top of the stairs, roll them down and collect them at the bottom. Needless to say, the speakers began to develop niggling little faults, like being totally useless, their

L–R: Paul Walters, Bob Dennis, Paddy Young, Neil Govier, John Walkie, Neil Dennis at the rear

cones smashed beyond repair. Mick left the band on a Wednesday evening. Having a gig on the Saturday, just three days hence, and unable to get a bass guitarist at such short notice, Neil Govier volunteered to play bass. A bass guitar was purchased on the Thursday and Neil set about learning to play the four-stringed instrument.

The Saturday night function was a success and Neil played remarkably well for one with such a small amount of experience. He became the band's bass player on a permanent basis, regularly reminding himself of drummer Dave Denning's words, 'Without a decent drummer and bass player, the rest of the outfit are wasting their time!'

Initially playing in and around Exeter at venues such as St Matthew's Hall, the Knight's Youth Club and America Hall in Pinhoe, Velvet Touch began to accept bookings farther afield. Covering the whole of Devon, Cornwall, Dorset and Somerset the band rapidly gained in popularity and were represented by the three leading entertainment agencies in the area, LMD, Starline, and Exonian.

A two-fold change in the band's line-up occurred in very short order. 'Big Neil' Dennis became ill from overwork, and drummer John Walkie was promoted by his employer and moved to Wales. Both lads were sorely missed, but the immediate problem of replacements was solved surprisingly quickly.

Neil Govier, who by this time had become an extremely competent bassist, also became lead vocalist, and the unexpected availability of long-standing friend Dave Denning made the departure of John Walkie somewhat easier to cope with. Four lads who contributed greatly to the success of the Velvet Touch were Ian 'Curly' Bartlett, Graham 'Udge' Hutchings, Robert 'Bob' Dennis and Ian Whiteway.

Curly and Udge were friends and supporters of the 'Touch', following the band's progress and watching their performances whenever possible. Taught how to erect and dismantle the equipment, the boys became indispensable. Bob and Ian, likewise, were supporters of the band, and in conversation decided that they would like to learn to play the saxophone with a view to joining at a later date. Both bought themselves a tenor sax, practised as if there were no tomorrow and were gradually incorporated into the set-up. Their induction into the band was probably the single most important change, both to the line-up and to the musical content. Tamla Motown and soul acts were regularly hitting the charts, and the newly incorporated brass section gave The Velvet Touch an authentic and contemporary sound.

The band frequently appeared at venues in North Devon, and strangely it seems that they were more popular in this area than in their own backyard. Making idle conversation with three girls following a dance in Barnstaple, one member of the band, who for reasons of domestic harmony shall remain nameless, asked, 'Where can we get something to eat at this time of the night?'

One of the girls replied, 'If you would like to give me a lift home and wouldn't mind dropping my friends off on the way, I'll get my mum to knock you up something.' Six musicians, two roadies, and the three girls climbed into the van, and after dropping two of the girls at their respective abodes, the rest eventually reached a remote farmhouse somewhere in the middle of Exmoor.

Leaving the apprehensive boys in the kitchen, the girl roused her mother who proceeded to cook eight cholesterol-packed fry-ups. Glancing at the clock, Neil observed that it was almost ten to four, then looked across the massive oak table at 'Paddy' and added, 'Better than Shirwell isn't it!' Usually, it was the facilities of tiny Shirwell, north-east of Barnstaple, that were a life-saver. Its garage, one of only a handful of commercial enterprises in the hamlet, had a coin-operated vending machine outside which dispensed hot and cold drinks, and a similarly operated petrol pump. The vending machine and fuel pump were extremely handy and frequently used by bands – musicians rarely had any money prior to a gig – and when desperately low on fuel, a detour to Shirwell would ensure that they made it back to base.

L–R: Neil Govier, Pete Jones, Phil Knight, Paul Walters at the front

Light refreshment, although from experience the author is unsure whether light is the correct word, after a local performance could be obtained from a 'hot-dog van' which was normally positioned just off the High Street in Exeter, outside Walton's store. The mobile eatery was a focal point for musicians returning home, and came to be known as Mother's.

The six-piece Velvet Touch, playing a blend of pop and soul, became one of the most 'bookable' bands in the South West with hundreds of followers. Often compared to Amen Corner and the Simon Dupree Big Sound, the boys were pleased to act as a support band for both these and many other big names including the Swinging Blue Jeans, The Yardbirds, King Crimson, The Bee Gees and Supertramp.

In addition to the 'support' jobs with the top touring acts, The Velvet Touch often double-billed with homespun talent such as The Graded Grains, The Codiaks, and The Variations. When Ian Whiteway left the band to pursue other avenues of interest, Alan Hart took his place. Alan, the proprietor of a vehicle repair business in Exeter, and Neil Govier moved into a house rented by members of The Empty Vessels until they left Devon to go to London, to become Wishbone Ash.

After an invigorating four or five years with the band, Bob Dennis moved to Wiltshire. When Alan Hart also decided to leave, the remaining members of The Velvet Touch suddenly found themselves bereft of brass. The departure of Bob and Alan heralded the end of the band. In consecutive months, Dave Denning left to get married, as did 'Paddy' Young for the same reason.

Drummer Pete Jones, and a keyboard-playing student at St Luke's Teacher Training College called Phillip joined the band, and The Velvet Touch continued to perform for a further eighteen months with a completely revised repertoire prior to disbanding, Paul Walters and Neil Govier being the sole survivors from the original line-up.

Paul Walters resolved to devote his time and energies to his 'proper job', and now runs a successful kitchen-fitting business. Neil Govier spent a few months 'depping' with local bands before being approached by drummer Ronnie Graham to play lead guitar with The River Set, a four-piece band comprising pianist Stan Gillick, double bass player Den Gunter, American vocalist Arthur Laurence and of course Ronnie Graham, which was the resident band at the Fisherman's Cot at Bickleigh.

Neil enjoyed three happy years at the Cot, the never-ending antics of Ronnie Graham causing each evening to be unpredictable. During his time with The River Set, Neil made many new friends and renewed old acquaintances with musicians who were 'standing-in' owing to illness or holidays. These included bass players Pete Evans and Dick Darlison, lead and pedal-steel guitarist Ray Hill, guitarist and saxophonist Alan Haydon, vocalists Dave Hoad and Tony Osborne, and drummer Pete Greenham amongst others.

In 1976 Neil was persuaded by a friend to audition for a lead guitarist's job with an Exeter band called Pride, who somewhat unusually featured two lead guitarists Ian Napper and Dave Wilson, the latter being the man whose departure was imminent and for whom the replacement was required. Neil auditioned, more out of interest than need, and was invited to become a member of the group. He joined Ian, drummer Bob Pengelly, bass guitarist Pete Snell and keyboards wizard Nigel Skinner, and it proved to be an interesting and satisfying move. The band played a good mix of music by bands like 10cc, Steely Dan and The Doobie Brothers, and was totally professional in its outlook.

Neil had completed no more than half a dozen bookings with the band when Nigel Skinner left. A hastily convened meeting of the group discussed the situation and agreed not to replace Nigel with another keyboard player, but with a brass section.

Advertisements were placed in Bill Greenhalgh's, the local press, and in one or two nationally distributed pop magazines. From the many applicants the band selected 'Taffy', an ex-serviceman who played the trumpet, and Bob Dennis, formerly a saxophonist with The Velvet Touch. The final change to what would remain a settled line-up came when Bob Pengelly left the band and was replaced by Ronnie Gleeson, an excellent drummer who had recently left an Exeter outfit called Buster.

All experienced musicians with a flexible approach, Pride quickly came to the notice of agents and dance promoters alike. The outfit remained uppermost in their minds after the band's appearance on the small screen. Pride answered an advertisement requesting local acts to audition for an ITV show called 'New Faces'. In conjunction with the Clevedon Management Agency TENK, Pride attended the auditions held in Bristol and won.

The boys featured on the show in May 1976, performed an original composition penned by Ian Napper called 'Everybody's Gonna Shout About It', and were overjoyed when they were again declared the winners. Pop legend Mickie Most, and Lionel Blair were generous in their praise and their marks reflected their comments.

Recorded on a Tuesday evening in the same studio as the soap opera 'Crossroads', the show was broadcast on the following Saturday. By all accounts, the switchboard at the studios of ITV Birmingham was inundated with telephone calls from agents, record producers and the like, to such a degree that a representative of Clevedon Management was asked to go to Birmingham to deal with it.

Neil Govier

Back in Exeter, the boys were contracted to open the brand new Woolworth store in the shopping precinct where they performed a number of short sets and signed autographs. Ironically, the band's success ultimately caused its downfall. There was much talk of the band turning professional and plans were allegedly being made for the lads to make a guest appearance on 'Top of The Pops'. This combined with a possible extended contract at a top club in the North East and a foreign tour, kept the band's management busy.

One or two members of the band were keen to become full-time musicians but the majority held steady jobs with realistic chances of promotion. The final decision decreed that Pride would remain a semi-professional unit.

Obviously the decision was not popular with those members who wanted to turn pro, and this created tension. The group as a unit eventually buckled under the pressure and Pride disbanded, having achieved, as they say, 'A lot in a little'.

The Whirlwinds also known as Formula 5

When Regimental Quartermaster Sergeant Harry Robertson of Her Majesty's Corps of Royal Marines was posted from Plymouth to the Commando Training Centre at Lympstone in East Devon, his son Douglas was sent first to the local infants' school, and later to the Exmouth Primary School in Exeter Road.

An intelligent boy, Doug passed the eleven-plus examination and went to Exmouth Grammar School. Doug made friends easily, and roamed the playground with Robert 'Bob' Jarvis and David Crowe, two similarly minded boys who liked girls and wanted to make music, or should that be the other way round?

Bob, or BJ as he would eternally be known, could play a few chords on his antiquated ukulele, and urgently needed more members to join him and trainee guitarist Dave in forming a skiffle group. Doug had been saving his pocket money for just this sort of 'rainy day', and decided that he too would get a guitar. Scanning the back page of the Sunday newspaper that same week, Doug spotted an advertisement for a company called Bell Accordions of Surbiton in Surrey who, according to the blurb, sold guitars as well as squeezeboxes, by mail order. A £14 postal order was sent off and his guitar arrived within a few days.

Bob told his new friend that he and Dave were members of the 5th Exmouth Sea Scouts and what with his dad being in the Marines and all, Doug ought to join up as well. 'It would be handy,' said BJ, 'We can have a group practice after the troop meeting.' Doug was enrolled into the Sea Scouts

The Whirlwinds entertain at Littleham Village Hall, 1962

5th Exmouth Sea Scouts' party

Arthur Pidgeon, Exmouth

with the blessing of both his mum and dad, and simultaneously became a member of The Bandits skiffle group, the name democratically chosen by BJ and Dave.

Ted Fullelove and Terry Mears augmented the trio, Ted volunteering to play a washboard that he had scavenged from Lord knows where, and Terry offering to play oil-drum bass, having been unsuccessful in his attempts to acquire a tea chest.

The Bandits' first public performance was at the Girl Guides' hut in nearby Budleigh Salterton. Dave Crowe had by this time found a tea chest and, although he was not the bass player in the group, he assumed responsibility for the 'instrument'. Arriving by bus at the Guides' HQ, Dave realised that he had left the tea chest bass at home. The other four members of the group

'Like the sweaters?'

were very understanding, and listened sympathetically to Dave's tale of woe and profuse apologies, prior to packing him off on the next bus to Exmouth to fetch it. Apart from this minor inconvenience, the evening passed without a hitch and the five boys had a really good time.

The little dance heralded several requests for the skiffle group's services. The Bandits played at youth clubs, church fêtes and the like during the next twelve months for organisations within the Exmouth and district area.

The Bandits 'split up' in 1959. For the second time in his career, Harry Robertson was posted to Malta, taking his family with him. However, the troubles in the Far East resulted in QMS Robertson being despatched to Aden, and his wife and son returned to Exmouth in the early part of 1960.

Back in Exmouth, Doug immediately contacted Dave Crowe with a view to getting the Bandits together again. Dave informed him that BJ had joined the Merchant Navy and that the others had all left school and were now working for a living.

'I've got a couple of mates who might like to start a band,' said Dave, 'Course it's all rock and roll now, not skiffle.'
'Great,' replied Doug, 'I'll leave it up to you then.'

Would-be drummer Colin Stuart, the owner of a snare drum and high hat, guitarist Phillip Vaughan, and a boy called Martin Webster joined Dave and Doug in forming the new band, named The Whirlwinds. Martin was a newcomer to the town and fancied playing the tea-chest bass, an item fortunately retained by Dave Crowe. Additionally, a first-class pianist, Michael Wymer, who had been professionally trained at the London Royal Academy of Music, occasionally played with the band, in what he describes as a vain attempt to 'inject a bit of culture into the proceedings'.

Surprisingly, this oddball mix of talent actually sounded good together. The Whirlwinds continued where The Bandits had left off, although this time round, they had the benefit of some stage experience, and a couple of musicians in Mike Wymer and Phil Vaughan, who could play exceptionally well.

At the end of 1960 Colin Stuart started work full-time, made new friends and found his leisure time to be at a premium. Dave Crowe had become disenchanted with the group, and Mike Wymer moved out of the district. Doug and Phil decided to form a new band, and were agreed that they should keep the name Whirlwinds.

Stuart, the youngest of the amazing Clarke family of drummers (brothers Gordon and Howard are both percussionists), Graham Lawrence – previously the bass guitarist with Barry Woodward's Graduates, and Bill Baker, a fourteen-year-old school friend of Doug Robertson and reasonable rhythm guitarist, supplanted the departing trio. With the exception of Keith

L–R: Mike England,
Stuart Clarke, Keith Vaughan,
Doug Robertson, Phil Vaughan

Richard Tarr, Exmouth

Vaughan, Phil's bass- playing brother who replaced Graham Lawrence some months later, the line-up remained unchanged throughout the life of both The Whirlwinds and Formula 5.

In the summer of 1962, Doug happily learned that his GCE A-level pass grades were sufficient to gain him a place at university, and in the autumn of that year he departed for the London School of Economics, reading Politics, History and Economics. At one of his tutorials, Doug was strongly advised by his lecturer to beg, borrow, or buy a textbook entitled *Samuelson's Introduction to Positive Economics*.

An advertisement on the notice-board in Doug's hall of residence offered a copy of this notable tome for sale at a cost of £2.10s.0d (£2.50), a fraction of the price when new. The seller was a second-year student called Michael Jagger. Doug contacted Michael, or Mick, as he preferred to be known, and bought the book over a cup of coffee in the Students' Union bar. The two chatted away and found that they shared a common interest, Doug being the lead singer with The Whirlwinds, and Mick being the front man for a band called The Rolling Stones.

Doug recalls, 'When Mick no longer came to the Union bar and had apparently 'dropped out' of school, I thought that he had probably got a job in a factory!'

In the notoriously severe winter of 1962/63, one dance at Starcross Youth Club was memorable for two reasons. Firstly, the blizzards that virtually brought the county to a standstill during that day, many roads being impassable, compelled The Whirlwinds to take their equipment across to the youth club by ferry, and remain there overnight. Secondly, the leader of the youth club, a Mr Holliday was so impressed by the band that he submitted their name to Westward Television for inclusion in a talent show. Roger

Telephone : Plymouth 66518

THE MUSIC CENTRE (Plymouth)
(Clarke & Chinn, Ltd.)
MUSICAL INSTRUMENTS   ACCESSORIES
SHEET MUSIC

Directors :   1 SHERWELL ARCADE
G. A. CLARKE   TAVISTOCK ROAD
O. M. CLARKE   PLYMOUTH

Business card: Clarke and Chinn

Gage, the programme director contacted Phil Vaughan by letter and invited the group to attend an audition at the studios in Plymouth. The Whirlwinds 'breezed through' the audition with all the lads in top form, and the brand new equipment, bought only recently from the Music Centre in Plymouth at very competitive prices, the proprietor being Gordon Clarke, the brother of drummer Stuart, sounded superb. Unfortunately, the band's television appearance was blocked because they were not members of the Musicians' Union, and could not join owing to their amateur status.

Doug continued to work his musical hobby round his university studies. Immediately after his last lecture on a Friday afternoon, he would hop on the tube to Waterloo Station and catch the train to Exeter. Another short journey by either bus or train, and he was back in Exmouth. This arrangement allowed The Whirlwinds to accept bookings for both Friday and Saturday evenings, leaving Doug to make the return journey back to London on the Sunday afternoon.

Notwithstanding the 100-odd miles that separated the other four members of The Whirlwinds from their lead singer and organist (Doug had purchased a Vox Continental organ following the recruitment of guitarist Bill Baker), the band still managed to rehearse, courtesy of the Post Office.

On hearing a song which he thought might suit both his voice and the band's style, Doug would write out the words, sort out an appropriate key, and send these pieces of information to Phil Vaughan who, with the other members of The Whirlwinds, would practise the number until they were happy with it. It was then reasonably straightforward to perform the number live when Doug next hit town.

The effectiveness of this system was proven by The Beatles' latest offering, a catchy song entitled 'From Me To You'. Doug heard the tune on the first day of its release (a Monday), and The Whirlwinds performed the song at Exmouth Pavilion on the Friday evening of that same week, at a dance where the three Exmouth groups at that time, The Graduates, The Royals and The Whirlwinds had been booked to play together in one show. It is believed that the door takings that night still constitute some sort of record for the Pavilion, with around 1013 people paying to enter!

In 1964, with no changes in personnel, The Whirlwinds became Formula 5. The reason given by Doug Robertson was that the new name sounded trendier and 'kinda cool'.

Cool: *Chambers 20th Century Thesaurus* defines the word as meaning audacious, bold, cheeky, and deliberate. In the truest sense of the word then, Miss Marlene Gillard was cool.

The Whirlwinds had been booked to appear at the St Margaret's church hall at Topsham near Exeter. The boys were met by the Revd Wilson, Mrs Wilson and a special constable. There had been trouble at previous dances, and it

Topless

AND AT THE CHURCH DANCE, TOO

By Daily Mail Reporter

EIGHTEEN-YEAR-OLD Marlene Gillard thought the church dance needed livening up. So she jumped on to the stage and started to sing. Then she unbuttoned her cardigan to reveal her home-made topless dress.

Youths who had bought 3s. 6d. tickets cheered as Marlene wiggled and sang her way through *Jailhouse Rock*.

As she finished, a flustered church worker warned her not to repeat the performance. Then he banned Philip Vaughan, 22-year-old leader of the Whirlwinds beat group, from allowing an encore.

'Smashing'

The dance was organised by officials of St. Margaret's Church, Topsham, Exeter. Extra precautions had been taken—a special constable was inside the hall—after trouble at previous dances.

All seemed quiet at 10.30 p.m. when the Rev. D. Wilson and his wife left for home. But then Marlene, a factory worker of Countess Wear, decided to do her act.

She said last night: "I thought it was a fabulous idea and I thoroughly enjoyed it.

"I wiggled and shook as I

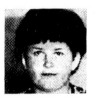

MARLENE
"*Fabulous idea*"

sang and the boys thought I was smashing.

"The girls said they admired me for my guts. But afterwards one of the Church organisers came to me and asked me to keep my cardigan buttoned up.

"My mother thinks the dress is disgusting and has threatened to burn it. But I can't let that happen, it cost me £3."

She added: "I think the church worker was upset because I wiggled too much—but that's dancing these days, isn't it?"

Choirmaster and organiser of the dance, Mr. Lionel Irwin, said: "There was a girl at the dance with what appeared to be a topless dress underneath her cardigan. But I never saw her take the cardigan off and it was a very orderly dance.

"There were about 250 kids there, mostly from our church, and had I seen anything indecent like this I would have thrown the girl out."

Philip Vaughan, of Exmouth, said: "Everyone was cheering and clapping the girl, but afterwards I apologised to the organisers because I didn't know this was going to happen."

At West Bromwich 17-year-old Mrs. Cilla Watts, of Wellington road, Handsworth, Warwickshire, got a £50 car for £5 after sitting in it for a minute while wearing a topless dress.

Garage manager offered the car at the knock-down price to the first woman who claimed it while wearing the new fashion.

At Weymouth, Dorset, a shop is selling topless night-dresses. And according to the proprietor, Mr. Godfrey Chapman, they are a top seller.

The buyers? "Half of them have been sold to men," said Mr. Chapman. "The others to women accompanied by men."

Cutting from the Daily Mail

was hoped that the 'Special' would act as a deterrent. The Whirlwinds tore into their first set at 8.30, to whistles and cheers from the 200-plus revellers.

At 10pm the band took a well-earned breather, returning to the stage twenty minutes later. At 10.30pm, the vicar and his wife thanked the band for their efforts and retired to the vicarage for their bedtime cup of cocoa, thus missing the impromptu cabaret.

Factory worker Marlene Gillard, eighteen years old and from Countess Wear decided that the dance needed livening up. Strolling casually to the stage, Marlene asked Doug Robertson if it was OK to sing a song with the band.

'Not a problem,' replied Doug, 'What do you want to sing?'

Accompanied by the Whirlwinds, Marlene began to sing Presley's 'Jailhouse Rock'. At the start of the second verse she slowly unbuttoned her cardigan to reveal her home-made topless dress. Marlene completed the song and left the stage to thunderous applause.

The *Daily Mail* of Tuesday 28 July, 1964, quoted Marlene as saying 'I wiggled and shook as I sang and the boys thought I was smashing. The girls said they admired me for my guts but afterwards one of the church organisers came to me and asked me to keep my cardigan buttoned up'.

Formula 5 were on the local scene until 1966 when Phil, his brother Keith, and Bill Baker left the band. Bill is to this day, convinced that he learned more about life with the band than he did at school.

Doug Robertson with The Ray Kent Combo

A Band of Absent Friends

Ricky Angus – bass guitarist – The Cougars

Stuart Boyles – bass guitarist – The Nightlights, Vic Palmer Combo

Ken Butler – drummer – The Deetones

John Carr – manager – The Variations

Terry Collins – lead guitarist – The Royals

Colin Drake – lead and bass guitarist – The Secrets, Four Steps Beyond

John Fewings – bass guitarist – The Corvettes

Ronnie Graham – drummer – The Vic Palmer Combo, the River-Set

Tony Harper – drummer – The Tornadoes, The Rejects

Alan Hempstead – trumpet – Sounds Tijuana

Maurice Price – drummer – Crescent City Stompers, Maurice Price Band

Norman Vautier – bass guitarist – The Corvettes

And sadly there may be more…

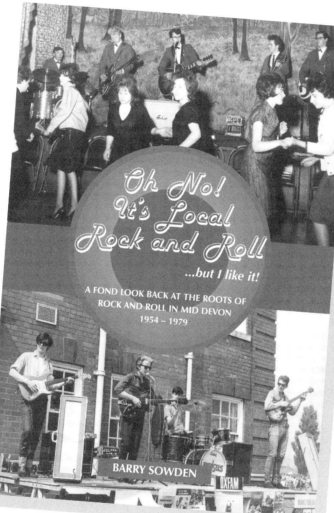